THE GREAT WALL

Compiled by Sun Zhisheng
Translated by David Lange

新星出版社　NEW STAR PRESS

Contents

Introduction

In the east of the world, on the length and breadth of China's soil, many earth, stone statured gigantic dragons rise. Among them is the gigantic dragon of the Great Wall, lengthen out to ten thousand Li. It leaves the Gobi, leaps the desert, strides the grassland and turns over the mountains. From the winding ups and downs of Yanshan it moves swiftly and descends. It faces Bohai, holds up its head and speeds along. Then it extends its head into the big sea, where it causes billows to surge and stirs waves every day, respires clouds and demonstrates its never exhausting vigor and enchantment. The Chinese people with all their heart and all their force took the totems within their heart to create it in their national territory. This is the Chinese Great Wall and the ten thousand Li Great Wall.

The children and grand-children of China, by toil and wisdom, with their lives and blood, started to construct the Great Wall. It not only includes more than two thousand years of politics, military affairs, economy, culture and important contents of other facets. It furthermore embodies mankind's mighty ability to create. It already has become a sign of a great work of art of mankind's historical civilization's height. Along the line of the historical Great Wall that stretches in an unbroken chain more than ten thousand Li long, there are countless constructions of in many ways designed passes, castles, towers, beacon fires. Rich and varied precious historical objects remain, that use different materials and different methods to create the mighty walls. It is not only an important material object for comprehending China's ancient military sciences, liaison contacts and building skills but also a ground of argument that can't be lacked when exploring the development of the economy and culture in China's north.

The Great Wall turns over high mountains, crosses gorges, goes beyond rivers and passes through the large desert. It can be seen as border wall and natural protection wall for China's agricultural and pastoral areas. It is an important foundation for studying ancient China's agriculture and animal husbandry, meteorology, hydrology and other sciences. The Great Wall is a rich treasure-house of culture and art. In the recent thousand and hundred years it was regarded as a subject for poetic masterpieces through the ages, fostering countless magnificent and graceful poems, producing countless stories that tug at one's heartstring. The Great Wall condenses the wisdom, blood and sweat of China's past working people of various nationalities. It ties a sacred link between all of China's ethnic groups and convincingly unfolds the historical progress of the form and development of the many ethnic minorities in China.

中国名片
CHINESE NAMECARDS

You can say that the Great Wall is like a more than two thousand years old encyclopedia of China that contains numerous known and unknown scientific contenst.

The Great Wall can be seen as a symbol for the Chinese nation and the pride of the Chinese people. Through the ages it has aroused lofty sentiments and aspirations of countless ardent men of high ambition who love China. At the same time it placed true feelings in the oversea subjects sentimentally attached to their motherland. It can be seen as a cultural heritage of mankind, attracting more and more good friends and personage from each and every country. Its eternal sublime value has already been generally recognized in the world. The ten thousand Li Great Wall will never fall down. The Great Wall demonstrates the glory of the creative ability and the human spirit that will forever dazzle our eyes.

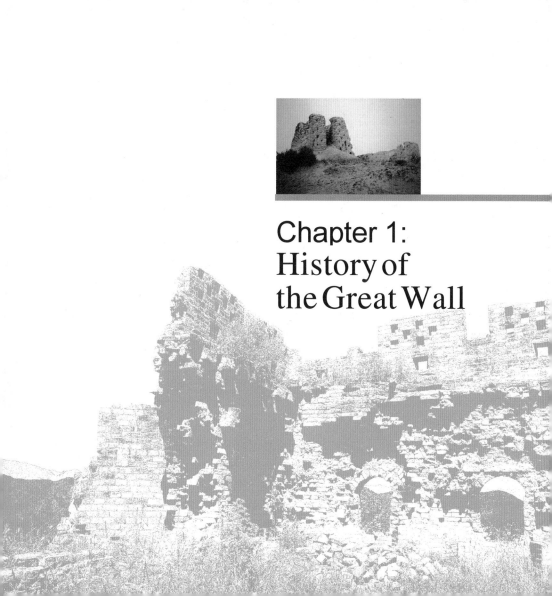

Chapter 1:
History of
the Great Wall

Chapter 1:
History of the Great Wall

The earliest Great Wall

When people discuss the Great Wall they often think about this uninterrupted, continuous wall, but that's not comprehensive. Actually the "Great Wall" is a scientific, continuously perfected ancient military devise for defense and an engineering setup. It not only includes that long wall that was constructed by piling up earth and stone, or the moats that were cut out of mountain ranges and river valleys, but also the castles, strategic passes linked and interrogated to the wall and the communication system of beacons in-and outside the wall. The first mention of the word "Great Wall" can be found in the records of the "Shiji", where in the article "Master Guan-Propriety" there is a sentence in the essay: "The Yang of the

Great Wall is Lu, the Yin of the Great Wall is Qi."
According to the lifetime of Guan Zhong and Duke
Qi Huan years of reign it can be inferred that the con-
struction time of this Great Wall (The Great Wall of
Qi) was between 685-645 BC. Moreover in the
"Shang-zhou chronicles" that recorded the state af-
fairs of the Spring and
Autumn period and the
Warring States period,
there is also an account
of Qi constructing a
Great Wall.

Concerning the ex-
plicit accounts of the
Great Wall, there is a lot
in the "Shiji" written by

the famous historian and writer of the Han dynasty, Sima Qian. He mentions that the states of Zhongshan, Wei, Zhao, Qi, Yan and Qin have built Great Walls and also mentions that the state of Chu has a "side-wall". "Side-wall" equals to Great Wall. Depending on documents and recordings, the earliest Great Wall appeared in the Spring and Autumn period. The construction of the Great Wall was no sudden emerging. From a distant perspective, it is "sealed woods" (using different sized fundaments of wood and filling it or covering it with earth) and "earthen city wall" (digging ditches and channeling water, raising the city wall by piling up earth) surrounding settlements of tribal clans or stockade villages in this remote and ancient period. Continuing from this setup of defenses the talk spread to nearby places. Since each of the

feudal lords of the Zhou dynasty established many
cities and towns, they spread the methods of "sealed
woods" and "earthen city wall" to the borders of
their land. In the Spring and Autumn period the military conflicts of the various states striving for supremacy became worse and worse. According to sta-
tistics of related material, there were more than 480
military actions of the various states in the year 242
of the Spring and Autumn period, among them a lot
of fights for offending or defending city walls and
moats. A lot of small states were destroyed because
their capitals had been broken through. The frequent
warfare strengthened the urge to build this kind of
resisting the enemy and safeguarding installations on
walls. The Great Wall of the Spring and Autumn period and the Warring States period emerged and be-

gan to develop under these kind of circumstances. About this point we can not only understand the Chu state's appellation "side-wall", but can also be enlightened by the writings of Mozi. Mozi can be seen as great thinker in the time of the Spring and Autumn period. He had put forward the "State preparation" as the center of the preparation for resistance thinking, and among one of the important parts is constructing city walls and moats as the core of the theory of constructing fortifications. This theory sums up the experience of each state in constructing city walls and moats and using them as defense. It also offers the first main source about putting up the Great Wall. In the complete and specific construction theory of Mozi the Great Wall is not explicitly being put forward, but from the practice of building the Great

Wall we can make out the profound and far reaching influence of the strategy and military tactics of defense ideas. The meaning why the "Great Wall" was named "Great Wall" in the beginning is probably also here.

The Great Wall of the Warring States period

As the history of China entered the period of the Warring States, along with the development of the circumstances, the seven powerful states adapted to the requirements of warfare, one after another vigorously constructing Great Walls. Among them worth researching are the Great Walls of the three northern states Yan, Zhao and Qin. The Great Walls those three states constructed all penetrated into the land of the nomadic tribes in the northern border region. And first they all had used armed force to open up the borderland and then built walls to resist. It are exactly the Great Walls of these three states at the northern boundary that lay the foundation for the later more than two thousand years history of the development of the Chinese Great Wall. A lot of causes and effects can be evaluated, but in fact it's hard for them all to thoroughly cast off the start with these Great Walls of the three states in the northern boundary. Why did Yan, Zhao and Qin put up long walls in the North? This has to be talked about considering the cir-

cumstances of that time. The Warring State period was a transition period from slave society to feudal society in the middle and lower reaches of the Yellow River and the Yangtze. The use of ironware was wide-spread, the development of productivity was swift and violent. Along with the economy between

the feudal states, political relations were strengthened and the trend towards unification became increasingly stronger. To adapt to the circumstances of that time, reforms were dynamically carried out and the seven powers of the Warring State period Qi, Chu, Yan, Han, Zhao,

Wei and Qin grew strong and prosperous and strived for going a step further with armed force and annex each and every state. At this moment the Jibei, Jinbei and Shanbei as well as other ethnic minorities of the Inner Mongolian grasslands began to grow big and powerful and started to establish ethnical political structures. At that time there were the Donghu at the northern border of Yan state. The Linhu and Loufan were in Zhao state's Northwest as well as the Chanlan and Xiongnu in its North. In the North of Qin state were the Yiqu, the northern part of the Yiqu were Xiongnu.

The Donghu, Xiongnu etc. were still in the phase of a slave society so they were similar to the societies dominated by slave owning cliques in ancient Greece and Rome. They were fond of looting neighboring

nationalities and countries in order to take their belongings and turn their people into slaves. To a certain degree the whole tribe seemed like a huge war machine. The skills of driving and riding horses were very high in these grassland nationalities and nomadic groups, they had a strong mobility. Because the Donghu and Xiongnu were very good at horsemanship and archery, they drifted between different places, were good at guerilla warfare and in their strategic upland they showed a very strong combat effectiveness. In the early stage of the Warring State period the troops of

Yan, Zhao and Qin still relied on infantry and war chariots. They wore loose garment with big sleeves. Through the influence of battle the three states had no choice but to conform to the current political situation of progressing reforms and undertake military actions to occupy the northern uplands. So they constructed as far as possible Great Walls in the territory where their influence reached most northern in order to prevent the Donghu and Xionghu from invading and harassing. In addition there were other Great Walls of the Warring States period for the purpose of guarding against invasions and harassments by their neighboring countries: the Qi Great Wall, the Chu Great Wall, the Wei Great Wall, the Zhenghan Great Wall and the Zhongshan Great Wall. The general trends and construction characteristics of the Great

中国名片
CHINESE NAMECARDS

Walls of the Warring States period constructed by the feudal states have basically already been clarified on the basis of materials from documents and modern archeological work and research by scholars. As for the Great Wall and the day when it emerged, it was not a simple wall, but it was separated into a part of mound wall (Wall platforms), where the troops defending it could live upon the wall. Along the line or in depth were beacon fires (Beacon towers), castles, constructed on passes were walled barriers. Thus it had the form of a complete set of engineering for military defense. You can also say that the Great Walls of the Warring States period already have built the frame for the design of the later more than two thousand years of the Chinese Great Wall.

The first ten thousand Li long Great Wall-
The Great Wall of Qin Shihuangdi

221 BC Qin Shihuangdi, by later generations called "the eternal emperor" succeeded in his politics. In a time span of not even ten years by relying upon his actual strength through expansions and accumulations of his ancestors and by displaying all sorts of strategies he successively destroyed the six feudal states of Han, Wei, Chu, Zhao, Yan and Qi. He established the first unified, multiethnic, feudal state with a system of a centralized government in the history of China and thus realized the first national assimilation. With the step and symbol of unification, Qin Shihuangdi issued a series of decrees, like abolishing the system of enfeoffment, establishing a system of prefectures and

counties, unifying Chinese characters, law, currency, weights and measures etc. and at the same time he put up the first ten thousand Li long Great Wall in Chinese history. Qin Shihuangdi constructed the Great Wall to guard against the Hu. Hu usually refers to the Xiongnu. While Qin Shihuangdi was campaigning for China's unification in the Southeast, the Xiongnu tribe in the North increasingly grew stronger. Their leader Manyu led the troops and occupied the Great Plains north and south of the large desert. Later he seized the opportunity when the garrisons in the North and West of Qin state were empty due to an attack on Chu state. He crossed the Yinshan Mountains and the Great Wall of Zhao state and the Yellow river, seizing its river bend and the territory to its East. On the western side he invaded the Qin Great Wall and plundered places like the Shang prefecture in the West and North of today's Gansu province (the Northwest of today's Ning county of Gansu province). The activities of the Xiongnu troops took place in a distant of only a few hundred miles from the imperial court in the capital Xianyang. This had to lead to a high guard of Qin Shihuangdi.

In the year 215 BC Qin Shihuangdi's Eastern inspection reached the Jieshi area of today's Qinhuangdao in Hebei province. Over there he ordered "Inspections by alchemists" and sent Lu Sheng, Han Zhong, Marquis Gong and Shi Sheng into the Sea to search for the immortals and the drug of

immortality. Soon afterwards he started an inspection tour to the Northwest from this place to the northern border area. Finally he went from the Shang prefecture (today's Suide county in Shaanxi province) back to the capital Xianyang (today's Xianyang city in Shaanxi province). This action undoubtedly gave Qin Shihuangdi a deeper understanding of the circumstances in the borderland and the situation of the Xiongnu's invasions. Just about that time the alchemist Lu Sheng returned from his diplomatic mission on the sea and reported about supernatural beings and supposedly presented a copy of a book from the immortals. Written on its top were the characters "the death of Qin are the Hu". We don't know if Lu Sheng thoroughly knew of the worries about the Xiongnu's invasions that weighted on Qin Shihuang's mind or if

Qin Shihuang had been looking for an excuse to attack the Xiongnu. In short, this event urged Qin Shihuang's decision to send his young general Meng Tian to lead troops in order to expel the Xiongnu that invaded the South.

In the summer and autumn of the year 214 BC he received order to lead an army of 300.000 men, divided into two routes. The main force went from Shang prefecture and passed through Yulin (today's Zhungeerqi in Inner Mongolia), entering the northern part of the Yellow River's bend. The other route of soldiers started from Xiaoguan (in the Southeast of today's Guyuan

in Ningxia province), entering the southern part of
the Yellow River's bend. Until the season of early
winter the troops led by Meng Tian had stormed and
captured Gaoque, Yangshan (Langshan in the Northwest of Yinshan), Beijiazhong (today's West of
Wuyuan, the North of the Yellow River bend and the
area south of Yinshan in Inner Mongolia).The
Xiongnu were awed by the Qin army's power and
retreated northwards. The borderland that originally
had been captured by the Xiongnu was completely
recovered. To guard against other invasions and harassments by the Xiongnu, Qin Shihuang ordered
Meng Tian's main army to continuously remain in
the border area and build the ten thousand Li long
Great Wall that started from Gaoque along the Yinshan
mountain range to Yunzhong (today's Tuoketuo

county in Inner Mongolia) up to Liaodong. Towards the southwestern direction they built the Great Wall from Gaoque along Langshan, Helanshan to Yuzhong (today's Lanzhou region in Gansu province) along the Yellow River, to protect the newly established 44 counties and the whole Yellow River

bend region. A lot of people from the inland were already moving to these 44 counties. Before Qin Shihuang had ordered Meng Tian to pursue the Xiongnu and construct the Great Wall, he had already been giving orders to raze the Great Walls of all the other states, although this razing wasn't thorough at all. As a unified country it could not be tolerated that there still existed many long walls inside the country, carrying the meaning of national boundaries.

To build the ten thousand Li Great Wall the Qin dynasty expended huge national strength and people's labor. Han Liuan told in "Huainanzi – Lessons of the human world" that Qin Shihuang drew 500.000 soldiers upon constructing the Great Wall. Among those sent to build the wall, were also so-called culprits who had not executed to burn their books within 30 days, "the ones that could not be corrected by law", and prisoners that were "intellectuals punished to shaved heads necks in chains". It can be seen that the punished ones who were sent to build the Great Wall or transport material to it were quite a few. There are modern scholar experts that estimate that the recruitment and employment of forced workers at the ten thousand Li Great Wall by Qin dynasty was "summing up rank-and-file soldiers, garrison soldiers and criminals were not less than several million people. The Construction of the Great Wall and garrison frontier fortresses by the Qin dynasty is inseparable. When Meng Tian led his 300. 000 men strong army to guard the line of defense in Hebei (today's northern part of the Yellow River bend), the garrison soldiers of others section of the ten thousand Li long Great Wall could not have been small in number. The garrison frontier fortresses were far away from the several million soldiers in the central plains and were not self-sufficient. They relied upon long distant transportation from the inland. Every transport that went out from the central plains carried 100 hectoliter grain; the defending forces in Hebei could only obtain half a hectoliter. One can well imagine the heavy burden for the common people to support them.

A folk song of that time told: "Give birth to a male, be careful that he won't be chosen. Give birth to a female, breast-feed her. Don't look beneath the Great Wall, there are skeletons leaning on each other". In July 207 BC a requisition of 700 men left for the Yangyu garrison in the North. On their way they were caught in the rain and stuck in Daze township of Qi county in Anhui province. Because they could not arrive on time they were forced to break the law, so they raised the righteous banner of opposing Qin. When the Qin court was finally destroyed in the burn-

ing anger of the big peasant uprising, the "Deeds of all ages" that Qin Shihuang had attempted, had only experienced two generations, existing only for 14 years. Even though Qin dynasty had been destroyed, the ten

thousand Li Great Wall constructed by Qin Shihuang can be seen as the first big symbol of unification that remained. In the evaluations of the people more than two thousand years later it still shows its effect and meaning.

The longest Great Wall —
The Great Wall of Han Dynasty

The Han carried on the Qin system, to lead everything under the heaven. The Han court took the defending of the northern border region and the Great Wall extremely serious. At the beginning of the Han dynasty when the country began to become stable, the social economy had not recovered and developed yet, and the Xiongnu, now under the leadership of

Maodun, defeated the Donghu in the East and the Yuezhi in the West, subjugating all neighboring tribes. They continuously invaded the Han border, robbing people, animal and property, wrecking production. Their military power appeared stronger each day. This resulted in the encirclement of emperor Han Gaozu at Baideng (This refers to the event during the time Liu Bang was a peaceful Han King and believed in collaborating with the Xiongnu, but they revolted and he was besieged by the Xiongnu army in Baideng mountain near today's Datong for seven days). Under these circumstances the Han imperial court had no choice but to suppress their anger and adopt the policy of "harmonious relations with their neighbors" and marry away girls of the royal family, doing their utmost to offer large quantities of clothes, food, weapons as tribute. The Great Wall was defined as national border in order to pacify them. But the Xiongnu still frequently crossed the Great Wall and carried out their invasions, the war between the Han dynasty and the Xiongnu continued. Until the time of Han Wudi

(Liu Che), seeing the previous experience and lessons and because the national power was strong and prosperous, he carried out two imperial conferences to discuss the matter, resolving in the adoption of a policy to resist resolutely. On the

one hand there were vigorous assaults, actively pursuing and attacking and station garrisons that grew their own food to garrison the frontier with armed forces to defend. On the other hand the construction of frontier fortresses at the Great Wall, establishing beacon-fires and defense works, made the Xiongnu lose their southern invasions and have the advantageous situation of " Big entries, big benefits. Small entries, small benefits." Thus they were in a condition of declining animal husbandry and scattered tribes. For this reason the Han with this strategy had no choice but to give up the area of Zaoyang county in the North of Shangyu where the Xiongnu were entering. This is also the reason why the Han dynasty had to retreat from route of the Qin Great Wall towards the South while constructing the Great Wall in the East.

The construction form of the military defense system of the Han Great Wall apart from the wall and the linked castles had lined walls, pavilions, beacons (signal-fires), obstructions, entrenchments, earth ridges, sky fields and banks. The structures that are being discovered at the moment show diversity in the entrenchments because of the different topography. There are approximately three types. One type of entrenchment can be found in mountainous and loess regions. The mountainous entrenchments are on one side heaped earthen ridges at relatively low mountain slopes, that's way these entrenchments are on the outer side. In plains entrenchments earth is taken on two sides in- and outside the entrenchment, so it has the shape of two trenches. Another type is the entrenchment of the Gobi and desert areas with heaped earth ridges on two sides. A different type is the entrenchments of river, lake or marshland areas, where a stop wall is built on the outer side. Concerning sky fields, it means spreading fine sand in entrenchments to inspect whether or not Xiongmu have crossed. Lang Zhonghou has summarized the methods of manufacturing:"Not all of the West Han Great Wall is made of earth walls, because of the cliffs there are stones, firewood is stored, and in river vales are floodgates".

In the time when the Han dynasty structured the engineering of the Great Wall's military defense there was a characteristic: they paid special attention to obstructs, stoppers, pavilions, beacons and set up a tight system of beacon-fires. According to the records of the "Ju Yan Han bamboo strips" there was the rule of "a beacon every five Li, a mound every ten Li, a fort every 30 Li and a town every 100 Li." in the Han times.

"The condition of the beacon-fires gazing into the

distant was astute in the Han frontier area, robbing the border area was of little profit for the Xiongnu." The Han dynasty took the early warning system of the Great Wall seriously, which allowed the royal court to set aside huge numbers of mobile soldiers that could be used for interceptions or assaults. Those big armies thus could be stationed in the inland and it could be avoided that violent soldiers betrayed their troops. This is a point of advance of the Han dynasty Great Wall compared to the Great Wall of the dynasty before. During the whole Han dynasty, especially during Western Han, they progressed repeated construction works at the Great Wall, shaping it to the longest strip of Great Wall in China's history. It started in the East in the area East of the Liao river, passing through the Yinshan mountains and the Hexi/

Gansu corridor. In the western direction it stretched
to Xinjiang, while at the same time strengthening the
defense north of the Yinshan mountains, adding constructions of two parallel outer Great Walls, adding
up to a length of 10.000 km. As the longest wall in
the history of the world, the Han Great Wall brought
into play a great value in both of aspects of defending against and attacking the Xiongnu. The Xiongnu
withdrew from the struggles at the steadily stretched
and tenaciously defended Han Great Wall and migrated towards the West.

Maybe it was because of the Xiongnu moving West
or the information spreading along the Silk Road
guarded by the Han Great Wall that the Roman army
in the 20ies of the first century AD built the Hadrian's
Wall between England and Scotland. The Hadrian's

Wall and the Han Great Wall share many resembling parts, although in length it did not reach one eightieth of the Han Great Wall. The English scholars David J. Breeze and Brian Dobson wrote in their 1976 published book "The Hadrian's Wall:" "The Hadrian's Wall is made of huge natural stone blocks. This caused people to think that when the Hadrian's Wall was built it received influence through descriptions of travelers about the Han Great Wall constructed two hundred years earlier." In the year 1900 the Hungarian geographer Jenõ Cholnoky, who went to China to observe and study, crossed the Great Wall and expounded the status of the Great Wall in the history of the world:"The Great Wall that developed to the West is the juncture of the intensity of power between China and the Xiongnu. That's why the Xiongnu's power collapsed after this setback, fleeing in disorder towards Europe, enough to violently shake the Roman Empire. With this meaning, although the two both became national dividing lines of political nature, comparing the wall of the Roman Empire with the Han Great Wall, one can really turn pale of shame."

The Great Wall constructed by the Xianbei nationality and Xianbei influenced dynasties — The Great Wall of the Northern Dynasties

The Northern Wei Great Wall

In the history of constructing the Chinese Great Wall there were not only Han ethnic dynasties to build the Great Wall. Dynasties of ethnic minorities also built the Great Wall. Among the earliest was the Northern

Wei dynasty that was founded after entering the central plains as host by the Xianbei people that had begun to develop in the North following the Xiongnu. In the times of emperor He of the Eastern Han the northern Xiongnu were defeated and moved westwards. The forefathers of the Xianbei moved from the West of the Xianbei Mountains to the old haunts of the Xiongnu in the North and South of the desert. Because they lived in the same place with the local Xiongnu people for a long time through intermarrying and mixing together, they formed such tribes as Tuoba Xianbei and Tiefu

Xiongnu. The Tuoba Xianbei called themselves descendants of the Yellow Emperor, appointed with the northern land. In the Xianbei language "Tuo" means "land", "Ba" means "descendants". The Xianbei people called the Yellow Emperor "virtuous king of the land", that's why they selected "Tuo" for their clan. During the period of the last years of Han dynasty, the Western and Eastern Jin dynasty and the Northern and Southern dynasties, the Xianbei became a dynamic force in China's North. In the year 386 AD the leader of the Xianbei nationality, Tuoba Gui, was enthroned in Niuchuan (In the Southeast of today's city of Huhehot). At the same year he moved to the capital Shengle (this old location is North of Tuchengzicun in the Northwest of Helin county in Inner Mongolia) and changed the dynasty's title into Wei, calling himself king of Wei, which was the beginning of the Northern Wei dynasty's foundation. 396 AD he moved the capital again to Pingcheng (today's Datong in Shanxi province) granting himself the emperor title, becoming Dao Wu Di, the first emperor of the Northern Wei dynasty. Thus the Northern Wei dynasty was established by the highest ruler of the Xianbei people.

In the "Wei book – Annals of Taizong" it is recorded that in the year 423 AD (the eight year of the era Taichang of Ming Yuan emperor Tuoba Si of the Northern Wei dynasty) "The Ruru attack places of strategic importance. In the second month of the fifth year of the sexagenary cycle a long wall in the South of the long river is built. It starts in Chicheng, reaches the five plains in the West and stretches more than two thousand Li, ready to defend." The Ruru are the

Rouran, in the historical records they are also called Rouru, Ruirui or Ruru (with different homophone characters). Ruru was the diction of how the Rouran nationality called itself. The Rouran originated from relatives of the Donghu people and composed of descendants from Xianbei and Xiongnu people, establishing political power in 402 AD. Its political center was set up in Dunhuang and Zhangye's North at the side of the Ruoluoshui. Afterwards the area of their activities continuously expanded, unceasingly invading into Northern Wei. The first emperor Daowu and the second emperor Mingyuan already often had to resort to arms on them. In order to guard against the Rouran and take precautions against the Khitan's harassments in the Northeastern region, emperor Mingyuan imitated the measures of defending against the Xiongnu during the Qin and Han dynasties. In 423 AD he constructed a Great Wall on the grasslands of Inner Mongolia, in today's northern part of Hebei province. In the East it started in the Northeast of today's Chicheng in Hebei province, passing Hebei's Zhangbei and Shangyi, entering Inner Mongolia's Huade, Shangdu, Chaoyouhouqi, Chayouzhongqi, Siziwangqi, Wuchuan, and Guyang, in the West entering among the Yinshan mountains with a length of approximately 1000 km.

Emperor Mingyuan passed away just after finishing this Great Wall. His successor Tuoba Dao, emperor Taiwu of the Northern Wei dynasty, installed six military garrisons on the line of the Great Wall to strengthen its defense of the northern territory and sent massive forces to guard critical spots. Distinguished from the West to the East these six garrisons are Woye (this garrison's local government is in the North of the five plains in today's Inner Mongolia), Huaishuo (this garrison's local government is in the Southwest of Guyang in today's Inner Mongolia), Wuchuan (this garrison's local government is in the West of Wuchuan in today's Inner Mongolia), Fuming (this garrison's local government is in the Southeast of Siziwangqi in today's Inner Mongolia), Rouxuan (this garrison's local government is in Xinghe in today's Inner Mongolia) and Huaihuang (this garrison's local government is in the North of Zhangbei county in today's Hebei province). In the period of Taihe in the reign of emperor Xiaowen of the Northern Wei dynasty, they also expanded the Yuyi garrison. In the beginning the seat of the local government of this garrison was in the Northeast of Guyuan county in Hebei province, later it was moved to the region of Dushikou. The Northern Wei, apart from building the wall and setting up garrisons in the northern part, in the year 446 AD (the seventh year of the Taipingzhenjun era) also requisitioned 100.000 men from Si prefecture (the seat of the local government was in the capital Pingcheng in the East of today's Datong city, controlling the prefectures in the capital's vicinity) and its neighboring prefectures You, Ding and Ji to build in Pingcheng on an area with a circumference of one thousand Li "an imperial obstruction enclosure" to encircle and guard the safety of the capital and the area under its jurisdiction.

After the Northern Wei dynasty broke up into Eastern and Western Wei in 534 AD, Eastern Wei once had constructed a Great Wall. The main part of the Great Wall was a repaired section of an old foundation of the southern ring of the Northern Wei's "imperial obstruction enclosure".

The Great Wall of Northern Qi

In the year 550 AD, the Xianbei influenced member of the Han people Gao Yang attained the position of prime minister of the East Wei, just like his father Gao Huan before, and was appointed with the title King of Qi. In the same year he abolished the Eastern Wei's Xiaojing emperor, approaching the emperor title himself, setting up a dynasty named Qi. He changed the title of reign to Tianbao, the capital as before was in Ye (In the Southwest of Linjin in today's Hebei province). In order to distinguish it from the Qi dynasty, established by Xiao Daocheng in the South of China who had overthrown the Liu Song dynasty, later historians called it Northern Qi. It was also called Gao Qi. To defend against nomads and the Western Wei (the later Northern Zhou), Northern Qi repeatedly constructed in the western and northern part the Great wall in the 27 years of its state founding, while attacks by formidable foes from the North such as the Rouran, the Turks and the Khitan were launched. The Great Wall of Northern Qi went through six constructions, joining together two lines. One line was on the exterior of the northern side. From Luyashan and Guancenshan in the Northwest of today's Shanxi province stretching towards the Northeast, passing Datong and Yanggao, in the territory north of Tianzhen entering the border of Chicheng county in Zhangjiakou of Hebei province, then along the Yanshan mountain range in southeastern direction passing Beijing, Tianjin and Tangshan's city area, entering the Shanhaigun area of Qinhuangdao city, until the sea. The other line is inside the southern direction. In the West it starts in Shanxi's Northwest in the area of Pianguan and goes to the Southeast. Reaching the North of Wu county it changes direction towards the Northeast, along the Hengshan mountain range, it comes to the East and enters Hebei province, it turns around along the Taihang mountains, proceeds northwards and joins together with the exterior Great Wall in the Northwest of today's Beijing city.

The Great Wall of Northern Zhou
In the year 557 AD the member of the Xianbei

nationality Yu Wenjue under the control of his step-father Yu Wenhu, a high ranking official assisting the ruler of the Western Wei, overturned Western Wei and founded Northern Zhou. Until the time of emperor Zhou Wu Di (Yu Wenjue's younger brother Yu Wenyong), Northern Zhou had experienced a period of strength and prosperity. In 577 AD they eliminated Northern Qi, unifying China's North. At that time the Turks, who were strong and prosperous in the North, continuously violated the border. In order to guard the borderland Northern Zhou continued the tradition of previous dynasties and constructed the Great Wall in 579 AD (the first year of the Daxiang reign of emperor Zhou Jing Di).

In the "Book of Zhou – Yu Yi's biography" it is recorded: In the beginning of the Daxiang reign, he payed a visit to the minister of education. Yi was instructed to inspect the Great Wall and establish defense works on the frontier. In the West it started from Yanmen until Jieshi in the East. He created new and changed the old, entirely achieving its strategic points in the clouds... Originally the Turks repeatedly plundered, now their residents are out of work. Yi used to have power, also patrolling by day. From then they did not dare to violate the border, the common people were in peace." "Jieshi" talked about in the document, are the "Meinüfen" rocks in the coastal waters South of Qiangzilicun of Suizhong county in today's Liaoning province, around 5 km East of Shanhaiguan.

The Great Wall of the reunified empire —
The Great Wall of Sui Dynasty

In 581 AD, not long after the ruler of Northern Zhou apparently requisitioned common people to build the Great Wall to protect the northern part from frontier troubles, a coup was took place within the imperial palace as the emperor's father in law the duke of Sui, Yang Jian, who had entered the palace to assist the ruler, abandoned the nine year old emperor of the Northern Zhou and declared himself emperor, founding the Sui dynasty. When he had unified China after nine years he ended the more than 300 years long lasting condition of division through multi-ethnic turmoil and thebstrive for supremacy since the last years of the Western Jin dynasty.

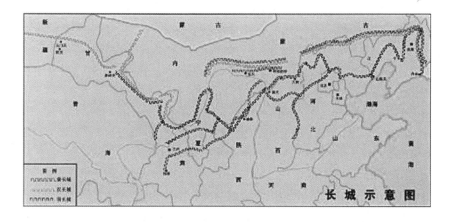

长 城 示 意 图

In the initial stage when Yang Jian was abandoning the Northern Zhou dynasty and establishing the Sui dynasty, the Turk leader Shabolue Khan who seized the North, used the request of his wife princess Qianjin for revenge, who had been married away by the Northern Zhou, as an excuse to continuously invade and harass the border land behind the Great Wall. The ruler of the Sui dynasty counterattacked the Turks' invasions and at the same time began to unceasingly build the Great Wall. After Yang Guang came to power as emperor Sui Yang Di, the constructions on the Great Wall did not stop as well. It is written in historical data and records that there were in total seven constructions of the Great Wall during the Sui dynasty. In the third year of the Daye reign (607 AD) when emperor Sui Yang Di constructed the Great Wall, because time was pressing, the people had to make gigantic sacrifices. The "Book of Sui" recorded that for construction of the Great Wall this time "more than one million male adults were sent out…When they stopped working after ten days, five or six out of ten were dead."

According to this calculation, in the ten days of this Great Wall construction more than 500.000 people died. The Sui Great Wall continued again after the Han Great Wall as a Great Wall of a big, unified empire and thus has a certain kind of function as is a link between the past and the future in the construction history of the ten thousand Li Great Wall.

The thousand Li long Great Wall constructed by the Goryeo state of the Tang dynasty

The Great Wall of the Sui dynasty that was built employing huge masses of people hindered the Turks from invading, but it could not stop the raging tide of domestic peasant revolts. Sui Yang Di's brutal and excessive campaigns that ran for years, forced people to revolt continuously. In the burning anger the Sui dynasty was destroyed and the Tang dynasty was founded. The national power of the Tang dynasty was strong and prosperous. Attaching importance on campaigning the borders were far outside the Great Wall. Consequently there were no large-scale constructions or increases at the Great Wall (In historical records duke Zhang of Yan says that in the first year of the Tang reign a section of the Great Wall was built in today's Huailai county of Hebei province). But in the early years of the Tang dynasty in the Northeastern region of Great Tang the Goryeo state occupied the old haunts of the Han Lelang prefecture and the ground of Liaoning a ten thousand Li long Great Wall was built to defend the Tang dynasty. It is said that Goryeo, originally named Goguryeo, is

another type of the ancient Buyeo that established
their political power in the last years of the Western
Han dynasty, using their ethnonym to name their state
while still being subordinate to the Xuantu prefecture of the Han. The earliest capital was founded in
Huanren (Huanren county of today's Liaoning
province), later it was moved to a city inside the country (Ji'an county town in today's Jilin province), Wan
capital (Near Donggou in Ji'an county). At the begin
of the fourth century they controlled the area of
Lelang county until they moved the capital to
Pyongyang in today's North Korea in 427 AD. During the period of the Sixteen Kingdoms when Qian
Yan once defeated Goguryeo, its state suffered huge
damage. After the Northern and Southern dynasties
Goguryeo had close contacts with all of the Northern

dynasties. When the Northern Qi dethroned the emperor in the first year of the Qianming reign (560 AD), the name was change to Goryeo.

The historical records write it that the Great Wall of Goryeo was constructed in the initial stage of the Tang dynasty. The people of Goryeo used Chinese characters to compile and write the Korean historical book "Chronicles of the three kingdoms (Samguk Sagi)" that records: "In the fourteenth year of King Rong Liu, in the second month of spring, the king moved masses of people to construct the Great Wall. From the city of Fuyu in the Northeast to the Southwest until the sea more than thousand Li, in altogether sixteen years the achievements were accomplished." In order to guard against the Tang dynasty's attacks, Goryeo from the fourteenth year of King Rong Liu (the fifth year of

Tang Zhenguan) until the fifth year of Ling Bao Zang (the twentieth year of Tang Zhenguan) spend sixteen years time to build a thousand Li long Great Wall in the direction from Northeast to Southwest. In that period "the king ordered the noble person of the West Gai Suwen to supervise the labor on the wall." The city of Fuyu's location at the Northeastern end of the Goryeo Great Wall is tried has been confirmed thorough research by present day's scholars to be on the second southern shore of the Songhua river within the Nongan county borders of today's Jilin county. In the Southwest it stretched to the seaside at Yingkou city in today's Liaoning province. In the middle it successively passes through Gongzhuling city of Jilin province, Lishu county and Liaoning province's Changtu, Kaiyuan, Tieling, Shenyang, Liaozhong,

Liaoyang, Anshan cities and counties.

The historical remains of the thousand Li long Goryeo Great Wall have already been blocked up and vanished. Experts believe that the section of the Ming Great Wall in the valley of the Liaohe has been built upon a part of the old foundation of the Goryeo Great Wall.

The ten thousand Li long Great Wall of the Jurchen dynasty — The Great Wall of Jin dynasty

In the twelfth century AD the Liao dynasty the Jurchen Wanyanbu leader Aguda rose in China's northeastern region, extinguished the Liao dynasty that had been established by the Khitan people was and founded the Jin dynasty. At the time the Jin dynasty was founding its state and opening up the borderland, the Mongols that were active in the northern Mongolian grassland gradually grew big and powerful, too. The Mongols appeared for the first time in records of the Tang dynasty, that called them "Mengwushiwei". At first they resided in the valley of the Argun river, later gradually developing westwards to the area of the Khentii mountains on the upper reaches of the three rivers Onon, Kherlen and Tuul. The strong and expanding Mongols continuously invaded the area controlled by the Jin dynasty. For this reason the Jin dynasty that had received Han culture, began to install castles, excavate trenches and afterwards linked the fortresses and garrisons and builded the Great Wall along the edge in the North where they came in touch with the

Mongols. There are no explicit records in documents that remained concerning the first years the Jin dynasty constructed the Great Wall. Historical circles believe that it started in the Tianhui reign of emperor Jin Taizong (1123 to 1135 AD) throughout the Dading reign, Mingchang reign until it was finished around the third year of the Chengan reign (1198 AD). Although there were still construction works afterwards, but these were all series of renovating, dredging and mending. The "History of Jin" and the "History of Yuan" call the Great Wall "Border fortress" , "Boundary trench", "Trench" or "Entrenchment", but don't call it "Great Wall".

The main part of the Jin Great Wall was built at the Hannan river on the route of returning soldiers from the war of Genghis Khan with the Jin state in 1204

AD, thus calling it "Genghis Khan border fortress". The Jin Great Wall historical remains of altogether nearly 5.000 km were again a ten thousand Li long Great Wall since the Qin and Han dynasty, built by the ethnic minority Jurchen state of China's North. The defense system of the Jin Great Wall was a composition of Great Wall trenches and border fortresses in strategic positions. The main structure of the Great Wall boundary trenches is made by digging an entrenchment, hindering war-horses from rushing or jumping over, inside thee entrenchments a long wall was constructed by piling up stones. At the main line of the Great Wall, other than at the branch lines, subsidiary trenches, subsidiary walls and platforms were added. There was also a difference in the design.

Compared to the previous dynasties, the defense system of the Jin dynasty Great Wall seems more perfected and applicable. Its trenches and walls stand side by side, making it able to defend against cavalry coming from grassland regions much better. The deployment of main and subsidiary walls side by side, the garrison forts and beacon-fires and the overall-arrangement is more reasonable planned. The Jin Great Wall went a step further in development to previous dynasties' Great Walls, so the Ming dynasty Great Wall could draw lessons from this experience and follow the old practice.

Collecting the achievements of previous Great Walls – the ten thousand Li long Great Wall of Ming dynasty

The ten thousand Li Great Wall built by the Jin dynasty and the successive Great Walls had not stopped the iron heels of the Mongolian cavalry. After the army led by Genghis Khan had destroyed the Jin dynasty he continued his military march to the South and attacked the West, establishing a Mongolian empire that stretched across the Eurasian continent. His son Kublai founded the Yuan dynasty in China.

The domain of the Yuan dynasty was vast, in- and outside the Great Wall traversing ten thousand Li, all was national territory. Moreover, the Mongolian people originally were horseback-people and in the North there was no form of other dangerous nomadic people. Thus there was no interest and need of further large scale Great Wall constructions. But the Yuan dynasty was a feudal dynasty established upon the oppressive basis of ethnic social status. The brutal ethnic and social class oppression stirred up an intense revolt among the entire Chinese. In the tempest of national uprising the Yuan dynasty was destroyed and the Ming dynasty was founded. The descendants of the Yuan dynasty retreated to the North of the Great Wall, entering a long-term phase of the Mongolian feudal lord and the Ming dynasty confronting each other.

To prevent a comeback of the Mongols the Ming dynasty, maintaining the rule over all of China, carried on long-termed and fierce warfare against various Mongolian feudal lords. After the middle period of the

Ming dynasty the Jurchen revived in the Northeastern area, continuously threatening the safety of the Ming dynasty's Northeastern border region. To consolidate the northern frontier defense the Ming dynasty during its 270 years of ruling China nearly never stopped constructing the Great Wall and managing the frontier defense. Adding up the accounts in the historical records from the beginning of Hongwu (1368 AD) to the end of Wanli (1563 AD) there have been more than twenty relatively large-scaled Great Wall construction works. The Ming dynasty Great Wall started in the East at the Yalu river in Liaoning province (the Eastern end is Dandonghushan), in the West to the East bank of the Taolai river in the Jiayu pass of Gansu province, traversing through the ten provinces, cities and autonomous regions of Liaoning, Hebei, Tianjin, Beijing, Inner Mongolia, Shanxi, Shaanxi, Ningxia, Gansu, Qinghai with an overall length of 8851 km. It is the most time-consuming, biggest engineering, most perfect in defense system and structure and the nowadays best preserved engineering project of the Great

中国名片
CHINESE NAMECARDS

Wall in China's history.

In order to strengthen the defense matters of the Great Wall and the commandment of the assigned troops along the line of the Great Wall and being able to frequently renovate the strategic passes, the Ming dynasty divided the line of the Great Wall in nine defend zones, called the "nine borders", the Great Wall was also called the "border wall". The nine border were borderland post headquarters in the beginning of the Ming dynasty, carrying out on the foundation of these post headquarters, according to the frontier defense terrain of that time the division of land was implemented and the principles of defending took shape. It took shape by the installment of a garrison as mark (army commander, governor commander). In the time of putting up the garrisons, all borders were in nonconformity. Probably only until the Hongzhi reign the installment of the nine borders' garrisons was completed. Because they were nine, they were known as the nine border key positions. Those nine border key positions were the garrison posts of Liaodong, Jizhou, Xuanfu, Datong, Shanxi, Yulin, Ningxia, Guyuan and Gansu. Apart from the nine borders and nine garrison posts, to strengthen the defense matters of the capital and protect the imperial tombs (today's thirteen Ming tombs) and the requirements for war preparation, the royal court of Ming in the Jiajing reign filled and set up the garrison posts Changping and Zhenbao in Beijing's Northwest. In the Wanli reign the garrison post Shanhai was separated from the garrison post Ji and set up. The garrison post Lintao was separated from

the garrison post Guyuan and set up, thus having nine borders and thirteen garrison posts. At the same time, starting in the Jiajing reign, the Xining guard in the East of today's Qinghai also constructed a "border wall".

The ten thousand Li Great Wall has some section that follow the practice of how constructions were carried out on the old Great Walls of Northern Wei and Northern Qi. New construction and building changed routes are not few, either. The Great Wall constructed by the Ming dynasty is not entirely fixed and constant. There are some section where in different periods there was progress, retreat and change. There are intervals of several tens Li. That's also the reason why there are place where up to now several strips of the Ming Great Wall exist at the same time. The emphasis was on the full use of the terrain by the garrison area and measures were suited to the local conditions, constituting depth and many ways of setups for constructing forts. That's a characteristic of the Ming dynasty ten thousand Li Great Wall developing towards a level of perfection.

The Ming dynasty ten thousand Li Great Wall can be regarded as the most grand and most perfect military defense engineering project in the history of China. During its continuous restructuring of the organizational system it took the shape of a complete defense system that was passed from the central political power to all levels of the military, the administrative body, joined basic military units and garrison soldiers defending cities. The defense works of the Ming Great Wall can be divided into garrison post towns (garrisons or the seat of a commanding military officer), road forts, guarding forts, pass forts, fortresses, barrack forts, fortified walls, walled platforms, battle towers, Yandun (Beacon towers) and so on in different ranks, alternative forms and buildings with different functions. They are linked, mutually coordinated or mutually conditioned to compose an integrated defense engineering system. Among them are pass castles of all sizes especially at strategic points. If you put the focus on the pass fortresses, which walls are linked to the Great Wall and form a little line of integration, a construction system to guard the line. It is another characteristic of the Ming ten thousand Li Great Wall developing towards a level of perfection.

From the Jiajing reign of the Ming dynasty and especially in the Longqing and Wanli reign, the large quantities of constructs on the walls possessed quite perfected installations of empty platforms for fighting and living (Kongxin Ditai), that went a step further in strengthening the Great Wall's defense ability. This is yet another characteristic of the Ming dynasty ten thousand Li Great Wall developing towards a level of perfection.

From the day the Chinese Great Wall began to emerge, all along more than two thousand years of continuous constructions. Before, a situation of constructing exhausting the whole nation's strength had been initiated. In fact, even with a unified empire in- and outside the Great Wall, as during the Tang, Yuan and Qing dynasties, renovations had not been called off at specific sections of the Great Wall (especially the Great Wall at important strategic passes and pass fortresses). Of course the main function was not national defense anymore but the territories' public order and the transporting economy.

After the People's Republic of China had been established, the People's Government attached a high level of importance to the protection, maintenance and the comprehensive utilization of the Great Wall. Among the directives, instructions and regulations to safeguard historical relics issued by the Central Government of the People and the competent department starting from 1950, all classify the Great Wall as a major project. Since 1952, according to the suggestion by famous historian, archeologist and writer Guo Moruo, receiving foreign visitors and the touristic opening up to the world was coordinated. The central government allocated funds to first of all repair the Great Wall at Juyongguan, Badaling and Shanhaiguan. Afterwards the Great Wall locations of Jiayuguan and Jinshanling were repaired year after year. In 1961 the State Council declared the three places of Shanhaiguan, Juyongguan Badaling and Jiayuguan the first group of national key units protecting historical relics. After that the key point Great Wall sections, pass fortresses and acropolis of the beacon-fires of Yumenguan Great Wall, Juyan (beacon-fires and frontier walls), Jinshanling Great Wall, the Xingcheng (Ningyuan acropolis)walls all were declared second and third group key units protecting historical relics on national level.

In 1984, at the time China was accelerating its reforms and opening to the world, the social support movement "Love our China, repair our Great Wall", launched by the "Beijing evening paper", "Beijing Newspaper" and the "Economic daily", started to unfold extensively. For this reason the chief architect of China's reform and opening, Deng Xiaoping, wrote down a dedication for "Love our China, repair our Great Wall". Following the appeal of this dedication, repair, renovations and new constructions were progressed on many key sections of the Great Wall with the funds allocated by the central government and money donated by the masses. Like the places of the Great Wall of Badaling Juyongguan,

Mutianyu and Simatai at Beijing, the Great Wall of Shanghaiguan Laolongtou, Jinshanling and Malanguan in Hebei, Huangyaguan Great Wall in Tianjin, the Great Wall at Jiumenkou and Hushan in Liaoning, Yanmenguan in Shanxi, Zhenbeitai in Shaanxi, Jiayuguan, Yumenguan and Yangguan in Gansu, and so on.

Among the contributors of money for the maintenance of the Chinese Great Wall are a lot of foreigners. These foreigners have already spread all over the world. The United Nations' UNESCO with the special international movement "Rescue Venice, repair the Great Wall" had contributed money and transferred it to Beijing city to repair a Great Wall section at Mutianyu.

The Chinese Great Wall that stands towering in the

East of the world for more than two thousand years. Some people add up its total length to not less than 50.000 km. The value of human civilization it includes emerged clearer along the time passed.

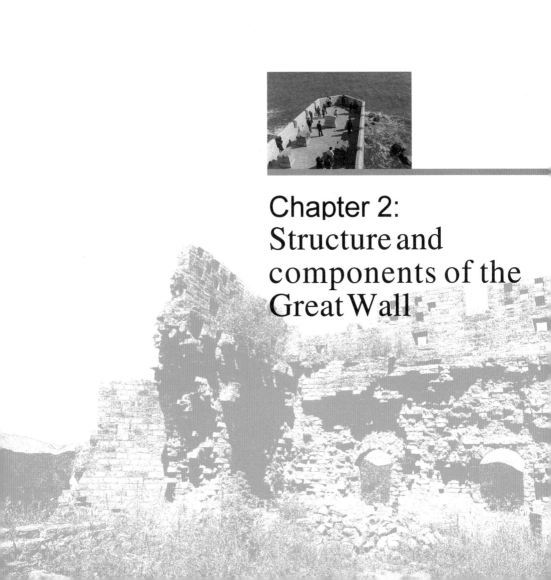

Chapter 2:
Structure and
components of the
Great Wall

Chapter 2:
Structure and components of the Great Wall

The Chinese Great Wall is the grandest and most long-termed complete military defense engineering project in the history of the world. The structure of its construction reflects the cold time of weaponry, when it received its function by people of a peasant tiller culture stopping nomadic cavalry from invading. If you scan every feudal dynasty in China's history

that built the Great Wall, the structure of their constructions shows differences because the level of construction technology and the economic power was not alike. But all share the basic three major parts of forms of Great Wall walls, Great Wall pass fortresses and Great Wall beacon towers.

The walls of the Great Wall

The walls are the most outstanding part of the Chinese Great Wall's construction system. The regular construction pattern of the walls, the types of structures, the material and the way of building all followed the differences of the ages and are not alike. Even walls of the same period, because of differences in the geographic environment and work conditions, each have distinguishing features and are rich and varied. Before the Ming dynasty all of the Great Wall walls were built with earth or stone layers. The brick layer walls of the Great Wall are a characteristic of the Ming dynasty and also indicate that the Chinese Great Wall constructions had already entered the peak time of perfection. Apart from the brick layer Great Wall, other forms of Great Wall wall constructions, although being improved during the more than two thousand years, yet the essential lasted all along and was constant, persisting on the principle "Suit measures to local conditions, draw on local resources." According to historical records and archeological excavations, according to the used con-

struction material the Chinese Great Wall can be more or less divided into: earth walls, stone walls, brick walls, brick and stone walls, strategic mountain walls, blast cliff walls and stockade walls.

According to the construction techniques, the Great Wall can be more or less divided into: the method of

ramming earth, the method of ramming earth in supporting boards, the method of piling up layers of sun-dried mud-bricks, the method of piling up layers of box-type flagstones, the mixed construction method of placing earth between flagstones, the mixed construction method of earth sand and plants, the mixed construction method of wood and stones, the brick layer method, the mixed layers of brick and stone method and the method of shoveling and cutting side slopes.

Because there were large quantities of brick and limestone in the Ming dynasty Great wall, there could be a lot of improvements, creations and innovations in its structure and form. Among the Great Wall brick walls there are types of war walls and barrier walls that had not existed in the past. War wall refers to a tall wall with eaves or a unilateral wall, with three ranges of shooting holes placed at the top, in the middle and at the bottom of the wall (there are also ones with two rows at the top and at the bottom). Soldiers deposited for defending the wall can use this brick layer wall to shoot out of a standing, kneeling

or lying position. The barrier wall refers to some lines of short walls that run vertically to crenel walls and continuously augment the construction on the inner side of relatively precipitous Great Wall crenels. These kind of short walls are approximately about two

meters high, about the same height as the crenel walls. The space of a crenel wall only allowed providing a narrow staircase for a single person climbing up or down. There were no observation and shooting holes on the wall. In this way, even if the enemy attack entered the wall, the soldiers defending the wall still could depend on the wall by steadily resisting. At the same time it could be avoided that the soldiers defending the wall lay bare in the enemy's line of sight or range of fire because of the precipitous terrain.

Of the same quality as the Great Wall walls are also the entrenchments. At the beginning of the time the entrenchments were developed, one side was a deep trench; the other side was the shape of a high embankment coming up from the turned soil. The height of these high embankments was usually about

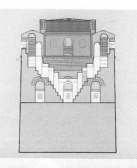

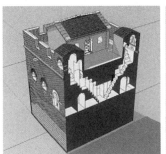

one Zhang, just like a high earthen wall. Because the trenches easily could be buried by sandstorms, that's why can see of the entrenchments today are often only the earth ridges. With relevance for the Great Wall walls are also horse-block walls and wall protection trenches. In general they all were constructed at frail places that are easy to attack and hard to defend and at the key places of different mountain tops. The so called horse-block walls are unequal stone walls constructed on the outer side of the Great Wall with a height of two to three meters, a width of two to four meters broad and a length from several tens of meters to over a thousand meters. Some used limestone brickwork filled with mortar, some were dried ramparts. One some walls corner platforms were constructed. The wall protection trenches are also called horse-block walls, they were constructed several tens of meters within the outside of the Great Wall. They are basically unequal trenches that in accordance with the Great Wall's alignment, excavated to a depth of two to three meters, a width of five to six meters and a length of several tens of meters to several hundred meters. Upon the walls of the Great wall there are some installations and structures that constitute an important part of the defense system.

中国名片
CHINESE NAMECARDS

Among them the wall platforms (Qiangtai) and enemy platforms (Ditai) are the most outstanding and important parts.

The wall platform is also called horse face, because it looks like the long face of a horse that stands out from  the walls exterior. The function of the wall platform and the enemy platform are alike. When enemy troops attacked, the defending soldiers mounted the platform to meet the approaching enemy. From the advanced position they fired down with projectiles, blunderbusses and cannons, making it unable for the enemy troops to approach the platform. If the enemy once was close to the Great Wall walls, the defending soldiers from the part of the wall platform that was standing out of the wall were able to shoot at the attacking enemy from the flank, eliminating them out of blind angle.

The enemy platform was also called "enemy building", in general points to high platforms standing out from the wall's outside and exceeding the wall, established on it in order to defend enemies attacking the wall.

The enemy platforms that can be seen on the historical Great Wall now, before the early staged of the Ming dynasty they were all "Shitai" (substantial platforms), meaning that by using bricks and stones or heaping earth "solid platforms" were piled up on the Great Wall, until after the Ming Jiajing reign the construction of "empty platforms" began. Empty platform means "hollow enemy platform". This type of construction was built when the famous Ming general Qi Jiguang, who had fought the Japanese pirates, was commander of the Great Wall of the Ji garrison during the era of emperor Longqing and Wanli. Those hollow enemy platforms usually were composed of the three parts of lower, middle and upper part. The lower part was the foundation, surrounding the center for the most part big stone band were used to build up layers. A few used bricks to build up layers. The interspaces were filled with earth and stones that were rammed. Its height was identical to the wall. The middle part was the hollow part. Some used brick walled pillars and brick layered bamboo tubes arches to bear the weight, building mutually connected arch rooms. Some used wooden pillars and wooden floors to bear the weight, on the outside enveloping it in a thick and heavy brick wall, shaping it into a relatively big indoor's space, thus providing a garrison for the soldiers and a deposit for rations, fodder and weapons. The upper part was the top of the platform. The top of the platform was surrounded by crenels. On the wall of the eaves beneath the crenels there were shooting holes, under the wall of the eaves the gutter was flowing. There were two types of organizational systems of platform tops: One type had a watch tower constructed in the middle of the platform top (also called observation pavilion). It could provide the soldiers guarding the platform shield from the wind and shelter from rain, when they kept a lookout. The watchtowers often

were one or three rooms Yingshanling style or Xuanshanling style constructions. There were relatively large-scaled watch towers of carrying Xieshanling style construction with a peridrome. Furthermore there were watch towers of Zanjianling style with a square façade. The other type had no watch tower constructed on it. By paving it with bricks or wood it was turned into an even platform. Wood was used to pave the even platform; to bear the weight wooden pillars were also used. Holes were opened out in the space between the floors so it could be used for rope ladders and wooden ladders to climb up

and down. Some only provided a brick layered flight of steps for passing up and down or passages of stone band steps going up and down. In the hollow place of the middle part arrow windows and doors were opened out. The two doors (the enemy platform's passing openings) all faced the Great Wall (there were some with only one door). On each of the two sides of the door a window was opened out (there were also windows that on one side of the door). The two sides standing out from the Great Wall's outside each had a certain number of arrow windows opened out. The fewer only had one, the most reached eleven. The majority had three or four. Most of the arrow windows were deployed in a row. There were also some that split in a stagger of two levels. The villagers near the Great Wall often named an enemy platform according to the number of its arrow windows on a certain side, like "three eyed building", "four eyed building", "five eyed building", "six eyed building" as far as "nine eyed building". There are also some places where "eye" is called "hole", calling them "three hole building", "five hole building", "nine hole building".

If you categorize on the basis of the function of the enemy platform and the progress of its inner structure, apart from special designs like circular shaped outsides, they usually all were square or rectangle. In general the four major kinds of single tube arch without pillar style, multi-tube arch with pillar style, ring-like tubes with pillar style and no tube wooden pillar floor to bear the weight can be divided. The tube arches points out that the depth

went into the direction of a structure with a relatively long scaled span of the arch. It was also known as shed arch. It used the lateral pressure between the building blocks to create a structure going beyond the empty stone body. Its bottom (with the space as its upper part) often appears as a semicircular shape or curve. In the hollow enemy platforms of the Ming dynasty, they often used brick layered tube arches to constitute relatively big spaces, providing the soldiers a garrison to rest, deposit rations and fodder, weapons and ammunition.

Because the Ming dynasty had hollow enemy platforms, it generated a "building army" that could guard the platform all year around. The historical records also wrote down that after the enemy platforms of the Ji garrison were established, Tan Lun and Qi Jiguang had recruited more than 9000 people of Zhejiang province to guard them. The building armies could take along their wife and children and could till and cultivate land near the tower. In the area of Dongjiakou, Damaoshan, Naziyu and Banchangyu in Funing county of today's Hebei province, there are the" Bao family building", " Gong family building", " Jiang family building", " Luo family building", " Zhang family building", "Wang family building", "Xu family building" and the " Fan family building" enemy platforms that have been named after more than ten kind of surnames.

The strategic pass castles of the Great Wall

Strategic pass castles of the Great Wall refer to the military defense castles that are connected to the Great Wall. Archeologists have discovered that on ruins going as far back as to the Qin and Han dynasty Great Wall there were little castles inseparable associated and interrelated with the Great Wall. The surface area of these castles is not big, the distance between the castles was unequal

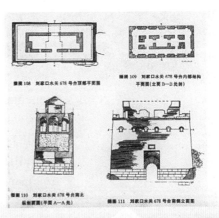

插图 108 刘家口水关 678 号台顶部平面图

插图 109 刘家口水关 678 号台内部结构
平面图(立面 B—B 处剖)

插图 110 刘家口水关 678 号台西北
纵剖面图(平面 A—A 处)

插图 111 刘家口水关 678 号台南侧立面图

中国名片
CHINESE NAMECARDS

several tens of Li. There were also small castles constructed in- and outside the Great Wall in the direction of developing in depth and breadth. In the Han dynasty those small castles were called "Zhang/ Barrier". The small castles a little big bigger than the "Zhang" were called "low entrenchment / Wu)". Stationed in those kind of small castles were many soldiers guarding the frontier. In the little big bigger castles, soldiers and civilians for the Tuntian/ self-sustaining station garrisons lived. In the Han dynasty, some of the Great Wall's strategic pass castles already were very famous and more-

over later became a synonym in the literature and art for the Great Wall strategic border positions. The Tang poetry for example frequently mentioned Yumenguan, Yangguan and Yanguan. In the history of construction the Chinese Great Wall there were some dynasties that may have not repair the walls of the Great Wall. But they had to repair the castles in the strategic border positions. Like the Tang dynasty that although not having any large-scaled repair works on the wall of the Great Wall, yet however delivered big strength in repairing the castles along the Great Wall of past dynasties.

According to historical records, during the entire process of constructing the ten thousand Li Great Wall, the construction of strategic pass castles by Ming dynasty continuously was in positions of first importance.

This not only displays in the construction in the early stage of the Ming dynasty's state founding first of all was every big strategic pass. It furthermore is shown that every time there were large-scaled Great Wall constructions, it was without calling off repairing and

new constructions at the strategic pass castles. The constructions of strategic pass castles of the Ming dynasty Great Wall in general can be divided in garrison forts (seat of a commanding military officer), guarding forts (seat of the commander of a certain level of military organized defense), road forts (the seat of a commander administering the roads below all garrisons), pass forts and fortresses of different grades, different functions and different form. Among these the pass forts and fortresses are the buildings of leading example. Some of the Ming dynasty pass forts inherited its scale from previous dynasties, some were newly established. They were the important stronghold to station troops along the line of the Great Wall and key points in guarding the Great Wall. The selected location often was on vital passages and thoroughfares coming in and going

out of the Great Wall. Once there were a lot o strategic passes on the Ming ten thousand Li Great Wall, like Fushunguan and Wuyaguan within the borders of present-day Liaoning province, Shanhaiguan, Jimenkou (with a common boundary to Liaoning), Xifengkou, Gubeikou (with a common boundary to Beijing city), Dushikou, Zhangjiakou, Zijingguan and Daomaguan within the border of present day Hebei province, Huangyaguan within the border of present-day Tianjin city, Juyongguan and Mutianyuguan within the border of present-day Beijing city, Pianguan,

Yangfangkou, Ningwuguan, Yanmenguan, Niangziguan, Pingxingguan and Guguan within the borders of present-day Shanxi province, Yulinguan within the borders of presens-day Shaanxi province, Zhenyuanguan and Sanguankou (Chimukou) within the borders of present day Ningxia Hui minority autonomous region and Jiayuguan within the border of present-day Gansu province. These pass forts, some of them now are already abandoned and some have already turned into vital traffic lines or touristic scenic spots. The structure of the Ming Great Wall's major pass forts in general are made up of rectangle or polygon walls, fort entrances, fort platforms, fort towers, turrets and enceintes of gates. Some have sieve walls and moats. The difference to usual prefectures and county towns was that it was more stable and more functional to be heavily defended. The big pass forts of the Ming dynasty often really were not just element of the defense facilities. The pass forts rather were its center, consisting of sieve walls, patrol walls etc., the near small pass forts, and the walls, wall platforms, moats, enemy building and beacon-fires surrounding it and composing a complete range of defense systems.

Along the lines of the ten thousand Li Great Wall

of the Ming dynasty many fortresses were established. There are many names of how to call these fortresses, like barrack forts, castles, border pass forts, mount forts and so on, including many small pass forts that are called. The circumference of fortresses usually was from about half a kilometer to one kilometer. The circumference of big barrack forts could reach up to two kilometers. The walls were both high and thick, there were one, two entrances, big barrack forts had many entrances. The fortresses were major points to station troops, they were the basic defenses strongholds on the Great Wall's defense line. There were also fortresses, were residents stationed at the border lived. In the Northwest they were called "military fortresses". The residents of the military fortresses frequently were assigned to tasks in renovating and

defending the Great Wall. There were also some fortresses that were established to let the villagers living
in the surroundings clear the fields and strengthen
the defenses when there was an alarm. In the endless
of history some strategic border fortresses of the Great
Wall lied waste and vanished, others evolved into
common villages. Some developed from simple military fortresses to the center of economy and trade of
its area, other became county towns sites and some
developed into preset-day cities, especially the several original garrisons forts and guard forts like
Datong, Xuanhua, Guyuan, Yulin, Wuwei, Zhangye,
Yinchuan, Shenyang (Shenyangwei) along with
Zhangjiakou, Beizhen, Jinzhou (Guangningzuotunwei)
all have already turned into famous big or medium
present-day cities.

Beacon towers (Duntai)

Beacon towers were an antique military warning and communication engineering installation, pointing at high platform constructions established on mountain tops, peaks or places from where you could watch each other easily and that were used to give alarm by kindling signal-fires.

Signal fires, also called beacon-fires, is an ancient kind of military measure of giving alarm. That is if enemies violated during the daytime by igniting smoke (beacon) and when invading at night by lighting fire (signal fire). The visible smoke and mist and the bright light alarmed the higher authorities of

each region. In the Han dynasty beacon towers were called beacon watchtower (fenghuo), pavilion beacons. The Tang and Song dynasties called it beacon platform, and also extended the word "beacon fire" to beacon tower. The Ming dynasty then called it Yandun/smoke mound or Duntai/ mound platform (In China's Northwest the Ming dynasty's big Duntai also had the function to resist the enemy, the small ones only had the function to keep a lookout, not lighting signal-fires). In general the distance between beacons towers was about ten Li away from each other, there was also the distance of about five Li away from each other in the Ming dynasty. When the soldiers guarding the platform discovered invading enemies, they immediately kindled the signal fire on the platform. After seeing it, the neighboring platform did the same. In this way the enemy's situation could rapidly be transmitted to the military central department. The appearance of beacon towers was not alike because of the time or because of the land.

In general there were two types, square and round. Beacon towers were constructed earlier as the Great Wall, but after the Great Wall had emerged, the beacon towers along the line of the Great Wall and the Great Wall closely formed an integral whole, becoming an important component of the

中国名片
CHINESE NAMECARDS

Great Wall's defense system. Some were even constructed upon the Great Wall, especially during the Han dynasty the imperial court attached high importance to the construction of beacon towers. In certain sections the continuous beacon tower constructions even replaced Great Wall wall constructions. The con-

struction of beacon towers along the line of the Great Wall was the same as the Great Wall construction, namely "Suit measures to local conditions, draw on local resources." In the Northwest many beacon towers were built with rammed earth, in addition there are some that piled up sun-dried mud bricks to construct them. In mountain areas many were built by piling up stones. On the part in the middle of the East since the Ming dynasty they were built by piling up bricks and stones or entirely encircled with bricks. In general the arrangement of beacon towers, apart from the one's constructed on the main line of the early phase Great Wall, can be divided in three types: One type is outside the Great Wall walls and stretches along passages to distant places, in order to monitor enemy tendencies. Another type is inside the Great Wall walls, linked together with strategic passes, places of garrisons or prefectures and counties, with the aim to promptly or-

ganize counterattack operations and strengthen defenses and clear fields. A further type is on the Great Wall's two sides (During the Qin and Han dynasty it had been constructed upon the Great Wall), in order to rapidly bringing the entire line of frontier garrison soldiers into play, rising to engage the enemy forces. In the early stage there were also beacon towers mutually linked to the capital, so that the imperial court as quickly as possible could be warned.

Beacon towers usually were single constructions.

About the beacons towers' structure and the practical condition, Han dynasty bam-

boo strips excavated among the beacon tower remains of Dunhuang and Juyan give an explanation: " four Zhang two Chi high, one Zhang six Chi wide, an area of 672 Chi." "One Zhang four Chi wide, five Zhang two Chi high." The Han bamboo strips also indicate

that there were five, six or ten number of people guarding the beacon tower; among them one person was beacon chief. Amon the garrison soldier one was in charge of keeping the watch, one had to prepare the meals. The others did repairs, collected firewood (including the firewood used when the signal fire was lighted) and works like that. On the whole there were six kind of warning signals, namely: Peng (Peng straw, there are scholars who believe that this were basket-shaped materials made by weaving woven or from textiles covering wooden frames), Biao (treetops, there are scholars who believe that this

are textile flags), drums, smoke, Juhuo (A torch made by tying together a shaft and a reed) and firewood pile (an elevated firewood haystack). During the day Peng, Biao or smoke were raised. At night, fire was lighted. The firewood piles and drums could be used both day and night. When lighting a signal fire, a thousand Xiongnu violating the border were taken as a limit. If altogether it were less than one thousand men, only one pile of firewood was burnt. When the number of men exceeded on thousand, two piles of firewood were burnt. When more than one thousand men attacked the defense works, three piles of firewood were burnt. Besides the firewood piles, different regulations were also attached to raising Peng, raising Biao and lighting the Juhuo. Because the positions of the invading enemies were not alike and because of the difference of day and night, all had different but very specific regulations. To guarantee that the beacon tower system was carried out strictly, the Han dynasty had a complete set of precise rules.

Until Ming dynasty, along with the high degree of importance attached to the Great Wall defense engineering and the mass application of firearms, the con-

struction and worked out styles of beacon towers also were improved. The message transmission and military intelligence of the Ming dynasty apart from releasing beacon or smoke, firecrackers were also set off. Furthermore when fire was lighted or smoke was released, sulfur or saltpeter was added to support the combustion. In the second year of Ming Chenghua (1466 AD) a decree fixed the methods of passing messages: "Fire first, if you see one, two enemies up to more than a hundred, light one beacon and set off one firecracker, for 500 men two beacons and two firecrackers; for more than one thousand men three beacons and three firecrackers, for more than five thousand men four beacons and four firecrackers, for more than ten thousand men five beacons and five firecrackers."

The most important function of the beacon towers was transmitting military intelligence. They had to coordinate close with other Great Wall construction such as enemy platforms and wall platforms. In areas with enemy platforms, they could act as mound platforms (duntai) and transmit beacon fire messages. In areas with neither enemy platforms nor wall platforms suitable to light a signal fire, beacon towers had to be established according to the route of the beacon fire transmission.

The construction components of the Great Wall

Building the Great Wall was a large-scale and arduous engineering project. Among the used construction materials, the important ones before the Ming dynasty were earth, stone and lumber. The Ming dynasty began to use large quantities of lime, bricks and tiles. Those used materials all were taken through the measure of

drawing on local resources. Stone was extracted up on the mountains . The stone construction material in conformity with certain standards was manufactured in nearby stone pits. There were some stone pits that not only manufactured Great Wall stone bands and various kinds of Great Wall stone components, but also manufactured defense weapons like stone cannons and stone mines. When the Great Wall was constructed in Ming dynasty, bricks, tiles and lime were used in great quantity; kiln factories were opened on spot to burn them. In recent years archeological excavations have discovered remains of brick and lime kilns on many places along the Great

Wall line, especially at a strip of Yizhen Great Wall. At some brick kilns also batches of Great Wall bricks that already had been burnt but not used yet could be unearthed.

The location selected for a Ming dynasty Great Wall brick kiln usually had to follow the principle of being close to water, close to earth, close to firewood, close to the Great Wall and exposed to the sun. Like this it was convenient for the Great Wall brick production to get earth, take water, collect firewood, form the bricks, let them roast in the sun and burn them. We can see from the archeological excavations of the

recent years that the Ming dynasty Great Wall brick kilns were a pit type of construction. This type of pit style kiln with earth walls that was excavated and constructed on spot was simple and small-sized. Thus they could be in accordance to the engineering project's requirements. When several were needed,

several were opened out. Because this was rather flexible, transport capacity could be saved. It was a relatively convenient and functional brick kiln, suiting the request of burning bricks in large quantities.

The construction components of the Ming dynasty Great Wall basically can be divided into the three major kinds of bricks, stone and tiles.

The Great Wall brick components: Brick is the main material of the Great Wall constructed in the Ming dynasty. The Great Wall's bricks are all black bricks and of silt or clay substance. Because the soil texture of every kiln is different, the amount of contained impurity in the bricks is not alike, either. But there were quality controls at that time. Bricks of incompatible quality could not be used for constructions at the Great Wall. According to design and purpose the

Great Wall bricks can be divided in long strip bricks,
square bricks and bricks with an unusual form. The
unusual formed bricks are buttress bricks, watching
hole bricks, shooting hole bricks, crenel foundation
bricks etc. Among the long and square bricks some
carry Chinese characters. The inscriptions on the

bricks basically show the brick making unit and time the brick was made.

Of Great Wall stone components there are principally Great Wall stone bands, crenel foundations, door post arch span stones, waterspout stones, door bolt hole stones, shooting hole stones etc. The stone substance is often sandstone or granite.

Fascinating is that on some door post arch span stones and door post stones, flower and bird, animal and cloud-like patterns, personages and writings were carved. For

中国名片
CHINESE HARDCARDS

example on a door post arch span stone of a Great Wall enemy platform in Funing Donjiakou of Hebei, the four characters "loyal and righteous dedication to the country" were engraved.

On the Great Wall houses and watchtowers were built, so there were tile items. The main tile components are concave tiles, barrel tiles, eaves-tiles (also called Goutou, round barrel tiles on the outermost end outside the eaves), dripstones (triangle concave tiles on the outermost end outside the eaves) and various kinds of tile items carrying beasts. There are many kinds of molded patterns on eaves-tiles and dripstones.

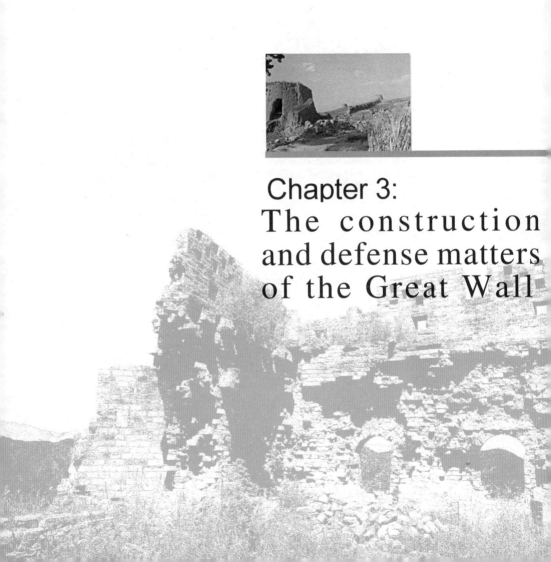

Chapter 3:
The construction
and defense matters
of the Great Wall

Chapter 3:
The construction and defense matters of the Great Wall

In more than two thousand years China has never stopped building the Great Wall and it all was constructed in the remote lands of China's North, where the signs of habitation were rare. The majority of places, if is not mountainous country then it is the Gobi desert margin area. There are places where the Great Wall was just constructed in the Gobi desert. Building the Great Wall it was necessary to use cubic meters of earth and stone in huge amounts. From the middle to the late stage of Ming dynasty, the emerging of the brick Great Wall required masses of bricks and lime. There were also the masses of Great Wall foundation stones, weighing over 500 kg. There

are experts who have calculated that only with the bricks, stones and cubic meters of earth of the ten thousand Li Great Wall constructed by the Ming dynasty a big wall could be constructed that was one meter thick and five meter high. This wall could surround the globe once and still had a surplus. Thus the huge volume of the engineering project can be seen. Today, as people have adopted modern technologies of movies and televisions, the Great Wall from a distant impression looks like a gigantic dragon that rises on the ridge of precipitous mountains, wriggles and cruises up to desert Gobi. Or one personally attends the scene and looks up at the Great Wall that has experienced many vicissitudes of life, yet still standing rock firm. Everyone will be shaken on account of the hardships, labor, lives, blood and sweat it's makers had to pay; astonished by the great creative power they showed!

The engineering project of the Chinese Great Wall is really too big.

Wanting to construct a large-scale and difficult engineering like this a precise organization and strong overall planning is undoubtedly needed for all the aspects of labor requisition, material sources, plan designing and construction work. You can say that this could only be achieved in a China with a high degree of autocratic centralization of power, prosperous reproduction of people and a flourishing peasant tiller civilization.

The sources of manpower for building the Great Wall

The primary source of manpower for building the

Great Wall was the army. You may also say that the army was the main force in constructing the Great Wall. When Qin Shihuang built the ten thousand Li Great Wall, he employed 300.000 soldiers sent to the North to garrison the frontier (in some historical records it are 500.000), and the logistic personnel serving these huge armies in this remote region were also quite a few. The Han dynasty Great Wall was often constructed by troops campaigning to garrison the frontiers, too. Employing troops to build the Great Wall shows an extreme prominence in the Ming dynasty. According to accounts in historical records, every time there was a large-scale Great Wall construction during the Ming dynasty, almost all frontier garrison defense forces were employed. Besides, one of the frontier garrison defense forces' main duties during peace times was repairing the Great Wall. Requisitioned civilian laborers were another important source for constructing the Great Wall. When Qin Shihuang built the Great Wall he conscripted approximately 500.000 civilian laborers. In the seventh year of Northern Wei 's Taipingzhenjun era (446 AD) for the construction of "imperial obstruction enclosures" 100.000 people of four prefectures were requisitioned. Eastern Wei also once had "Called 50. 000 workers from four prefectures to build a wall in the Northern mountains". In the sixth year of the Tianbao reign of Northern Qi (555 AD), when the inner Great Wall between Juyongguan and Datong was constructed, they called up 1.8 million civilian laborers. The Northern Wei once "sent all people to the East of the mountains to built the Great Wall", too. The Sui dynasty repeatedly built the Great Wall, almost every time they had to requisitione male adults. Among them was one time in the third year of the Daye reign of Sui Yang Di, when more than one million were requisitioned for only ten days time, more than half of  them dying through the labor. Because the male adult population already by far was not enough to apply on the various kinds of forced labor, finally even widows were conscripted to go constructing the Great Wall. In the Jin dynasty's Chengan reign prime minister Wan Yanxiang was excavating boundary trenches. When he began to apply he said: "I request to use foot soldiers to pierce trenches and build barriers." As a matter of fact it were "soldiers and civilians laboring equally, moreover refugees were hired to attend duties, after fifty days it was accomplished." When the Ming dynasty constructed the Great Wall, they also requisitioned civilian laborers. A little progress was that the peasant worker constructing the wall had a little payment in the Ming dynasty. For example in the fifth month of the 16thyear of the Jiajing reign, inspector-general of Zhili and supervising censor Wang Ying in a document to the ruler had mentioned that at the time several section of the Great Wall in the Juyongguan area had been constructed " altogether 695 bricklayers, every worker for work and food received eight silver fen, in all 55 tael six cash."

Culprits banished to frontier garrisons to serve at the border were the third source of manpower for the historical construction of the Great Wall. In the period of Qin and Han dynasty, there was a special kind of punishment, called "Chengdan", which was punishing criminals by sending them to built the Great Wall. Among the labor forces constructing the Great Wall there were many punished convicts until the Ming dynasty. In the fifth year of the Lonqing era (1571 AD) the provincial governor Yang Zhao put forward in his reserch. In other words, the number of years served as a sentence were equivalent to the amount of construction at border engineering. After accomplishing the task, you were released and could return home.

Principles and methods of building the Great Wall

For the last two thousand years, the Chinese people displayed great architectural skills when completing a tremendous project like the Great Wall. Not only by implementing the principles of "Dealing with danger of topography when building fortification" and "Use local material for building and defeating" they also showed great knowledge on the organisation of the construction area, the allocation of the material etc.

"Dealing with danger of topography when building fortification" is the basic principle while constructing the Great Wall and has been followed accurately for more than two thousand years. It has been implemented because it reflects a strong ideal of China, the special topography of north china and the approach to the Great Wall. When researching for the building of the Great Wall people already discovered that the Great Wall in fact displays the boundary line for the nomadic and

agricultural civilization. Within the last two thousand years this boundary line experienced changes and development. But however it changed, it always took in advice the specific conditions of the northern Chinese topography. Compared to the earlier Dynasty, during the Qin and Han Dynasty, the main strategy was building from north to west. However, after the Han and Qin Dynasty the Great Wall marked the crossing zone of the nomadic and the farming civilization, namely from Da Xing An Ling, Yan Mountain, Yang Mountain, He Lan Mountain, and Min Mountain to Heng Duan Mountain. From north to south just is the area that you can call "Govern with the danger of topography". By using the crossing zone as a defending barrier, the Great Wall itself isn't only a defending construct but for military use, but also can storage a maximum limit of material and people. As a huge and accurately planned building, the construction of the Great Wall was very meticulous. Nowadays, most of the Great Wall that visitors can see is build upon the mountains, particularly on their ridges. No matter if it is bricks, stones, blast cliffs or difficult mountain terrain: from outside the wall looked steep and hard to climb but from inside actually was flat and easy to climb. The critical points where especially when passing the narrow gaps and rivers between

two mountains, and also when building the important infrastructure on the open land. The man-build Great Wall and the canyons being natural defending barriers are a very close combination and again reflect the principle of "Govern the danger of topography".

"Use local material when building and defending" is another very important principle in the construction of the Great Wall. Because of the vast span of the Great Wall of China, the unequal time consumption regarding the construction of each part of it and the very short time frame, the principle "Use local materials when building and defending" also displays another importance, namely on the basis of construction methods and even military weapons. The height, the thickness, the length, the material quality, the position of the beacon tower (Yan Dun) and its shape all without exception embody the principle of "Use of local material when building and defending". The ruins and stone pits along the wall side near to Ji County as well as the stone inscriptions are a very good example for this.

Building the Great Wall is a very complicated and tight project. According to historical notes, the construction of the Great Wall has been divided and assigned into smaller segments and districts. Whenever critical situations occurred, the central government sent out troops and labourers to assist in the building process. In particular cases the organization was in charge of the military forces. The construction of the Great Wall was complying with the segmentation into four regions in Han/Chao Dynasty (Wu Wei, Zhang Ye, Jiu Quan, Dun Huang) and was organized by the county officials of these regions. The county officials then gave authority to every district's garrison soldiers. In the early years of the Ming Dynasty, the construction of the Great Wall was lead by the military forces and their respective jurisdiction. Afterwards, more emphasize was put on maintaining the construction process and clear division of work and methods. According to documents and inscriptions on the Great Wall, by that time the construction of the Great Wall was lead by every district's military general (it was often the military inspector of the province, who was send out directly by the emperor, or the military head of each county). The military general was expounding to the imperial government the defence situation of every part of the wall at any time as well as giving recommendations on the construction process of the Great Wall. Only after receiving the opinions of the imperial government, the construction could be further organized. At the construction site, the staff was divided into supervisors and specific construction staff members. The supervisors were mostly high ranked officials, like military inspectors of the government,

head supervisors, commanders and military generals, while the construction staff consisted of organizers and below general managers. During peaceful times, within the military staff was divided into so called military teams ("As a farmer, first do the farming when you arrive back home"), namely a spring and an autumn team. The spring team being sent out from March to august and the autumn team from September to February respectively, patrolling alongside the Great Wall they were of great use to the construction of the Great Wall.

During the Ming Dynasty, the allocation of responsibility was very clearly. To ensure quality in the construction process of the Great Wall, after Long Qing the method of carving the producer's name on the weapon (incurving the names of the construction units and staff members onto a board) and thus determine the organization management. Archaeologists and Great Wall Experts discovered and collected some stone inscriptions. These stone inscriptions recorded every step of building the Great Wall (including enemy broadcasting stations), its places, lengths, heights, widths and also the names of the official titles of the supervisors, designation of the military unit, organizers of the construction site, stonemasons, bricklayers, carpenters, ironsmiths, and pottery makers. Only because of the strict organization management system, the Great Wall in Ming Dynasty could withstand hundred's years of hardship and "by being strong and firm ensure the people's peace" letting people experience the atmosphere of this wonder.

Most part of the Great Wall was built on steep mountains and in deep and serene valleys. And even if there was flat land, most of it was desert, therefore the transportation of material was very complicated. According to legends historical notes, there were basically three types of methods transporting the material:

The first and most important one is relying on

manpower. Every piece of stone, clay and wood and the later used brick, lime etc. has been transported by men using baskets, carrying poles or simply carrying it uphill on their shoulders. Those days, in almost inaccessible areas, it was very difficult to create lines in order to lift the materials up the mountains. During the winter, the ice covering the soil was used to pull and push the material up to the mountains to the construction sites.

The second method was the easiest one of all. By using all kinds of vehicles (different vehicles in different dynasties) and the methods of battle logs, claw bars, capstans, (winches) and also within deep valleys the usage of "connecting two cliffs with a cable and transport material into baskets from each cliff to the other", the material was loaded into baskets and on thick ropes smoothly drawn uphill.

The third method was using animals to transport the material. Since the Great Wall was built on steep cliffs, it wasn't easy for the people to climb up the hills, more important, they didn't need to carry heavy material on their back. Also, legends say they were using goats and monkeys, e.g. putting lime and other material into baskets and buckle it on the back of the monkeys and brick and other material on the back of goats. With this method, transportation problems were solved easily.

When architects were building the Great Wall hundreds and even thousands of years ago and therefore encountered technological problems, they showed great knowledge and skills when facing them. The adopting of architectural skills and methods even lets people nowadays marvel and admire, for example the levelling of hillside fields was a very complicated and craftsmanship-needed task. Stacking up stone bricks inside the enemy broadcasting stations in order to construct splendid vaults, archways, doors, windows and sweeps all until the very day make the Great Wall the most abundant, artistic and practical exhibition of craftmanship.

The Great Wall and the defence

Within the different stages of building the Great Wall, every ruler throughout the dynasties, whether or not advocating the building of the Great Wall, couldn't neglect the use of the Wall as a defence object. And in peaceful times the Great Wall was of good use to the economic growth, ensuring traffic flow and a harmonious civilization.

When preparing for war, the military forces of the Great Wall put together an army of soldiers, garrisons in order to be more effective. The administration zones and districts along the defending line were also combined together to unify the country and deploy a masterpiece-strategy to become the toughest and most perfect defence system in ancient times.

Before reaching its peak in the Ming Dynasty, the defence of the Great Wall experienced changes and development throughout every dynasty.

For guarding, commanding and observing of the

Great Wall during the Ming Dynasty, boarding lines alongside the Wall have been established and divided into nine districts (altogether consisting of nine districts, later thirteen). Each district was again divided into several districts called "Lu" and was led by a general.

All strategic passes were merged together, every street passage guarded by a post and every pass observed by "garrisons on duty" or low positioned "Qian" and "Ba" officers The total amount of soldiers depended on the specific circumstances and thus determined.

When talking about the defence system of the Great Wall one cannot neglect the garrison soldiers, who where occupied in border line settlements, barriers and castles. This situation was kept until the Ming

Dynasty. In the Ming Dynasty, those places weren't called "settlements and barriers" anymore but "mound", "pass", "camp", "castle" and so on. Until the later stage of Ming Dynasty, garrison soldiers still lived in the enemy broadcasting stations.

During the Ming Dynasty, these soldiers that have already been stationed for many years alongside the Great Wall, were called "main soldiers". Those soldiers in case of urgent circumstances being able to move to other regions and be bound for military services were called "guest soldiers". At the same the "vassal had to inspect the boarder alongside the wall every autumn". Later on, during autumn, the guest soldiers that were being transferred to the boundaries to defend were called autumn-defence-soldiers.

After fourteen years of peaceful autumn and the

completion of the construction of the walls in Ning Xia, troops were being posted alongside this wall (its former name is strong defence) to guard in the so called "Bai Bian", a special type of walls.

In the early years of Long Qing, when the county of Tiao Li was in charge of discussing military affairs and Qin Ji Guang started the reformation of the defence system, constructing hollow enemy broadcasting stations became an important measure. and set a system putting into practice the basic guarding principles of the enemy broadcasting stations of the Great Wall. Therefore, the former guarding practice of just posting guards at camps and castles and not guarding the sidelines of the walls has been changed and main- and guest soldiers were unified. According to historical notes and archaeological studies, firearms were already deployed for defence purposes. Qin Ji Guang also implemented vehicles and equipped them with firearms. During the time of Ming Jia Jing, the guerrilla warfare tactic has been implemented and military actions were supported by coordinated actions of the "guerrilla soldiers".

In short, the defence system of the Great Wall of China due to its different times and places constantly gone through changes and followed only one basic principle: "Building the Great Wall according to the topography and provide support with coordinated actions.

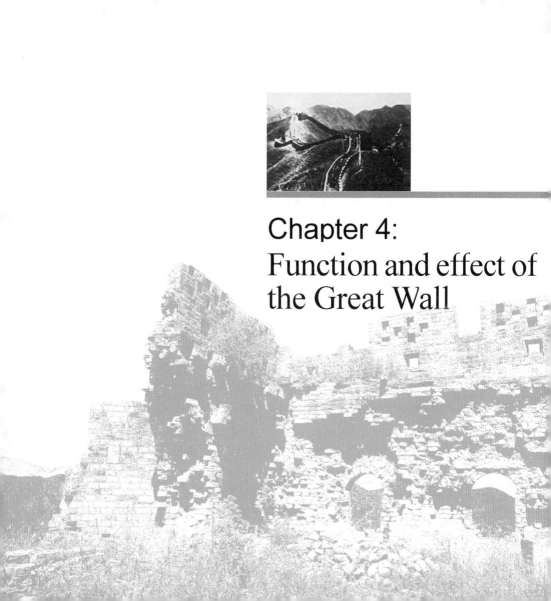

Chapter 4:
Function and effect of the Great Wall

Chapter 4:
Function and effect of
the Great Wall

The rock-firm standing Great Wall in the North of China is without a doubt a tremendous military defence project and greatly reflected the military functions over the last two thousand years. However, with the progress of time other functions and effects of the Great Wall start to become visible. For those people truly understanding every function and effect of the Great Wall, research on the Great Wall has a very important meaning.

The Great Wall and its military defence functions and effects

Throughout Chinese history and during the period of Jian Shao in Han Dynasty, the physician Hou Ying was the first one on expounding a system on the function and effects of the Great Wall. In the book that he reported to the emperor were mentioned ten remarkable reasons. As a matter of fact, these reasons were about the functions of the Great Wall and its construction. From the article of Hou Ying one can see that people two thousand years ago and earlier already knew of the Great Wall not only as a defence wall against the invasion of the Xiong Nu ethnic group, but also as a prevention against people fleeing. Concerning this and what following people and even people nowadays neglect is the fact, that the Great Wall perceived this two functions ever since two thousand years ago and earlier. It is also these kinds of functions showing us that the building of the Great Wall as a defence line has been implemented out of political and military motivations and at the same time was the connecting tie between the two people behind each side of the Great Wall.

Five centuries afterwards Gao Lu, a writer from the imperial court of the Xian Bei ethnic group published a book called, in which he analysed the wriggling landscape of the North of China as being a risk to the integrity of the country with its boarders and also expounded the building of the Great Wall and its history.

He also summarized the five advantages of the Great Wall:

Here, one has to take into consideration that the ruling class at that time was the Xian Bei ethnic group, which actually were nomadic people. After taking over the political power and the building of the Great Wall, they didn't only adopt political systems of the agricultural people but also adopted their defence system with its principles and methods and, as nomadic people, started to build the Great Wall as a vast defence system against the other nomadic people, the Rou Ran.

The question of how to improve the effectiveness of the military defence functions of the Great Wall has been elaborated quite intensively by the military. In the second half of the Ming Dynasty, the imperial

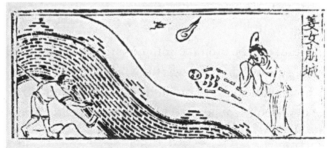

court again declared that building the Great Wall and its strategic passes is a factor of favourable landscape and yet needed the cooperation of the emperor's counsellors and brave warriors in order to strengthen defence and, most important, by all means improve the precau-

tions and awareness of war in peaceful times, avoid slack and the neglect of one's duties. Only by (setting up the defence of the Great Wall) effective defending could be achieved. This deeply summarizes the thoughts of the military defence throughout the dynasties in which victory or defeat lied upon the capa-

bility of investigation knowledge.

When it comes to the defending oneself against the enemy history already reveals that the invasion of the Xiong Nu ethnic group could be stopped in Qin and Han times. During the northern dynasty the invasion of the Rouran tribe could be stopped from the south; in Tang Dynasty had the function to defend against the possible danger of the Tu Jue tribes; in Jin Dynasty the Great Wall withstood and stopped the attack of the Mongolian military forces. During the Ming Dynasty the Great Wall was of effective use in order to stop the plan of the Yuan emperor from taking over influence and power. It also numerous times smashed the plan of the Late Jin emperor to break-through the Great Wall and attack and capture the capital.

During history, the Great Wall was of great success in stopping enemy military forces from invading and exploiting the country. Regarding this matter, lots of historical notes could be found during Ming Dynasty. Qin Ji Guang for example built a solid part of the Great Wall in Li County and successfully repulsed the attack of Tartar's cavalry and summoned.

The Great Wall as its whole construction is very clearly a defence construction. The Ye people (Jurchen) in Ming Dynasty, who rose from the north and slowly entered the country from west ahd to be actively defended against by the imperial court. From far west building two corridors fierce fighting has been started and the imperial court repeatedly had to send out high ranked guards. Under the situation of not being able to enter strategic passes, the enemy forces tried to bypass them and enter Beijing by sea and over the mountains. The Qing military forces successfully passed some strategic points of the Great Wall and entered several regions as Hebei, Shanxi, Shandong etc., threatening the capital's safety and provoking the state of the "the capital as prohibited area".

However, even though the forces were able to achieve some victories, they never invaded important strategic regions and only "came to plunder". The reason for this was just what Wei Yuan wrote down in his about the strategic districts of the Great Wall, namely "controlling the strategic passes on land

and sea in order to avoid drawing near power and influence from outside. Which means entering from different passes, surrounding and blocking my way out." In the end, the forces were able to control the central Chinese plains and commence a new era of Manchurian ruling the Chinese country. From the military point of view, the cause could not be seen in the insufficient function of the Great Wall as a military defence barrier but the military general Wu San Gui, who rebelled against the Ming but surrendered to the Qing.

The Great Wall broadening infrastructure in North China

North China was a desolate and out-of-the-way area with insufficient infrastructure. But with the building of the Great Wall as a military defence barrier and the connection of every of its guarding points in order to improve the defence and ensure fast gatherings, strong military presence when needed, and transporting material and army provisions, a complete infrastructure system has been set up in the northern territory and for the purpose of the inspection of the boarder defence line by the emperors, broad roads have been built. Not only the paths alongside the Great Wall were main transportation arteries (as it has been praised as the "silk road" later on, being an important communication line in the east-west) but also inside the country numerous roads have been built (as lots of points for smoke and fire signals have been set up according to the paths and roads). As a matter of fact, the Great Wall itself is just one line of infrastructure the military uses to communicate; most parts of the Great Wall could be reached by foot fast and easily. In order to serve as a path for migrants within the new economy zone with its roads on the wall, besides the wall, and offside, the Great Wall became the infrastructure system. Under the aspect of being a defence system and ensur-

ing the smooth flow of people and goods, the infrastructure system of the Great Wall made another step in contributing to a solid boarder defence and economic development alongside its walls.

Today, we often say the Great Wall has been built to protect the "Silk Road". Actually, in the early days of the Silk Road, the Great Wall hasn't been established out of "exchange" or "trading" needs but rather because of military needs. Following the construction of the Great Wall, quietening of wars, the people's security, and economic development, "exchange" and "trade" have emerged flourishing as time demanded. Originally constructed as a defence barrier out of military demands with roads built specifically used by the military, the Great Wall became as a part of the Silk Road the communication line between the central Chinese plains and the west. At the same time, the Silk Road faced development under the protection of the Great Wall. In the history of China, the Silk Road alongside the Great Wall has never been given up and the rise and fall, the Silk Road has gone through during the Tang and Han Dynasties was always connected with the Great Wall as the defence barrier. Even when key places of war moved to the north east and the beginning of the Ming Dynasty with its prosperous overseas Silk Road (the capital during Ming Dynasty was no longer Xi'an in the North-West, but Beijing in the North-East), the

north-western part of the Great Wall still contributed to the protection of the Silk Road and its corridors on the west-side of the river. By that time, the Silk Road with its countries outside Jia Yu Guan in the area of Xi Yu established wide-ranging trading connections with the imperial government of the Ming Dynasty. When paying tribute to the emperor, after entering Jia Yu Guan the tributes from Xi Yu were escorted by the military to ensure their safe arrival. Some tributes were brought into the capital directly by the people. In the era of the Ming Dynasty, the Silk Road and its tribute paying to the emperor has never been broken down under the protection of the Great Wall. It is because of the tributes paid to the emperor, that the imperial government of the Ming Dynasty was able to strengthen its economic ties, deepen the friendship with all countries of the Xi Yu Area, and isolate the power and influence of the Yuan Dynasty's rulers in order to maintain peace at the boarder area of the West and the East.

The influence of the Great Wall on the infrastructure was also visible in terms of water transport. In order to maintain the transportation of pays and provisions for the soldiers on time, besides using the Grand Canal new canals were built and seaways explored. At that time, the part of the Great Wall that runs into the Sea, also known as Lao Jing Tou, was an important sea transportation region.

The symbolic meaning and evolving awareness of the Great Wall

Since the starting day of building the Great Wall it has become the unifying symbol of the Chinese people. For more than two thousand years there have never been thoughts of separation about the Great Wall, therefore it could also never separate the Chinese people themselves. As a military defence construct, the Great Wall naturally became a symbol of the military, national defence, solidness and security of the country.

Taking a sweeping view into history, the Great Wall is a symbol of the Chinese people and has been accepted by all Chinese, especially during the period of the Second World War and the anti-japanese war. At that time, the Japanese as an insular people, flagrantly invaded China and enslaved the Chinese people in the occupied areas, having the pipe dream of annexing China. By stepping on it, the Japanese invading troops used the Great Wall as their symbol of victory. Facing the peoples' death and at the same time looking at the Great Wall as the symbol of national defence, peoples' unification and naturally the Chinese peoples' unification, aggression and resistance appealed to every single Chinese people. The war of resistance against aggression in 1933 revealed the first page of the heroic story of the anti-japanese war. "Swear to survive or perish with the Great Wall" became the common oath of the anti-japanese war. "Resist becoming slaves and build anew the Great

Wall with your own flesh and blood!" *The March of the Volunteers* voiced the aspirations of every Chinese people. "The ten thousand Li long Great Wall, outside of it is my home——the whole Chinese people unify as the ten thousand Li long Great Wall" *Song of the Great Wall*, similar to the power of inspiration unleashed the patriotic enthusiasm of hundreds of millions of Chinese people. *The March of the Volunteers* later on became the national anthem of China. Whenever people hear or energetically sing the anthem they feel a sort of patriotic passion, which lies in the sympathy of hundreds of millions of Chinese people that the Great Wall evokes.

Similar to other great ruins in the history of mankind, the Great Wall gradually turns away from its military meaning to a cultural spirit that constantly heightens a two-way history evolution. Charmingly and aesthetically, it reveals the intelligence and creativity of the Chinese people on the side and the strong will and imposing manner of mankind on the other side.

So it is because of its strong charm and aesthetic that it attracts the whole world. To some extent the world takes the Great Wall as an example in order to truly understand China. The first time the Great Wall being mentioned in western literature was probably in the book "History of the decades", written by the Portuguese historian de Barros and published in 1563. In the book was written: "What I heard so far regarding the Great Wall, I believed it would never be consistent. But after this map, it is consistent. I'm quite surprised." De Barros, nevertheless, never went to China.

In September 1793, G. Macartney came to the summer residence in Re He (now Chengde, Hebei) as the envoy of King George the 3rd to have an audience with the emperor of the Qing Dynasty, Qian Long. When they entered the Great Wall from the ancient North Entrance, they could see the part of the Great Wall which was later portrayed in the copperplate etching "Chinese scenery" . This copperplate etching truly depicted the flexuosity of the riffs when walking on the Great Wall. In the foreground are two officials sitting in sedan chairs, a team of attendants and natives waiting for the attendants, in the background is the Great Wall. This piece deeply affected the impression western people had about the Great Wall. On September 5th, 1793 Macartney wrote down in his diary: "If the whole Great Wall is the same as the part that I have seen, this is without a doubt the most tremendous architectural piece that mankind has created with his one hand so far. I think, even if one collects every stone in the world and piles it up to build a stockade, it could never compete with the Great Wall of China." " By building the Great Wall the ancient China shows, that it is not only an extremely strong empire but at the same time also consist of intelligent and deeply moral people. In order to decide building such a defence barrier for protecting their descendants, the Chinese people have to be at least very far-sighted people and care-taking to their offspring. They even invested huge amounts of labour and wealth in advance to avoid the descendants facing dangerous situations."

70 years after Macartney praised the Great Wall, the german archaeologist Hillmann published the

book *My Journey to the Great Wall*, a book highly praising the Great Wall: "The Great Wall is without a doubt the most astonishing piece of work mankind has ever created with its own hands. It is a tremendous monument remaining from the past." Hillmann knowledge of the Great Wall wasn't comprehensive. He believed the part he saw was that of the Qin Dynasty not the Ming Dynasty. But the impression his work gives the western world still remains today. When Europeans come to China they want to climb the Great Wall and be inspired by it.

The Hungarian archaeology student Stein who was drawing a map of the chinese Xi Yu region for the English empire also did investigations on the great wall on its western part out of Han Dynasty. In the book "Archaeological Notes in Central Asia by Stein" he published in 1933 (translated into chinese in 1936) he also mentioned "I cannot but marvel at the technical skills chinese architects possessed in ancient times", "these military and architect specialists were facing fierce natural difficulties and revealed their persevering spirit in organizing power to again create a striking proof.", "feel that the power of the chinese people by finishing the Great Wall, the quick advancing policies in the Han Dynasty and the sacrifice and suffering of the people were all of great impact", "to be frank, this can be seen as a victory of the power of spirit over material things."

At the time when Western people continuously deepened their knowledge about the Great Wall, there were also some Chinese able to free themselves from tin influence of history and reveal new knowledge about the Great Wall. This kind of knowledge was mostly expressed throughout poems. In the period of Kangxi in1694, Chen Zhang wrote the book *Moving out from west*, when the Great Wall already lost its military function. At that time, numerous poems of this kind have been written, one can say a new era of knowledge started. During the period of Kangxi Emperor the governmental officer Pan Qi Can wrote "Visiting the fortress of the guards at the stream outlet"(1717) in which he summarized the historical meanings of the Great Wall in the Ming Dynasty, Emperor Qian Long, who frequently came into contact with Westerners wrote the poem *Great Wall*. His view on the Great Wall became the main trend of knowledge during the Qing Dynasty; the Great Wall is a magical architecture but guarding the country was still implemented by "De Hua". One person being able to give an impartial evaluation and new knowledge about the Great Wall was the official Ma Xun (1828), his *Song of the Great Wall* was the longest poem ever written in the ancient times of the Great Wall. It not only contributed to the history of the Great Wall, praised its majestic appearance but also revealed a new meaning of the history of the Great Wall. After Ma Xun the Great Wall showed its imposing appearance as well as its culture for thousands of years and will never be extinguished.

Besides its military aspects and knowledge about it, Chen Tian Zhi during the period of Qing Emperor Kangxi also pointed out the recreational value of the Great Wall. He said, Lao Long Tou, where the Wall ends into the Sea, with its Cheng Hai building on top.

The work reveals that he also sees the Great Wall as a recreational area and therefore the importance of protecting and maintaining its state.

In modern China there are two people influencing generation after generation of Chinese with their evaluations of the Great Wall. One of them is Sun Zhong Shan, who pointed out that the Great Wall "is the most renown building on the soil of China", "a great building, a unique world wonder."

The other one is the great writer Lu Xun. He wrote a very short passage called *Great Wall*: "Tremendous Great Wall! When Lu Xun says the Great Wall is "great" and at the same time "cursed", it is in fact a literary comparison. Lu Xun uses the Great Wall to compare culture and system of feudalism. Thooroughly eliminating the feudalistic system is a very formidable and at the same time hard task.

No matter how people where evaluating the Great Wall and its symbolic meaning in the past, the Great Wall became a symbol of the Chinese people, naturally formed throughout history. People all over the world could identify themselves with the Chinese struggling against the invasion of Imperialism, especially when fighting against the Japanese invasion.

During the 26th General Assembly of the United Nations the Peoples Republic of China recovered its legal seat in the United Nations. The gift from China to the United Nations was a knitted tapestry draft of the Great Wall. This again reveals the great identification of the Chinese People and the Government with the symbol of the Chinese People, the thousands of years old shining Great Wall. The whole world can accept and identify itself with its symbolic meaning. In 1987, the UNESCO added the Great Wall to its World Cultural Heritage List and thus marked a new era in the world's acknowledgement of the Great Wall.

The cultural meaning of the Great Wall is not only characterized by its strong people, but also rooted in the pursuit of the true, good and beautiful similarity of earth by mankind and being intoxicated with it. At the 2nd International Meeting of Architects and Technicians of Historical Sites in Venice May, 1964, the *Charter of Protecting and Restoring International Historic Sites* pointed out: "Throughout centuries, peoples' historical sites were filled with ancient information and became the witness of people's lives in ancient times until now. People more and more realize the value of the unity of mankind and see the remains as a common legacy as well as the responsibility of protecting these historical relics." Because of the increasing knowledge of the Great Wall, the international community better understands and identifies itself with those values. From 1954 until now almost 500 State leaders and Government Chiefs visited the Great Wall of China and expressed their heartfelt appreciation, e.g.:

In 1972, the 2nd of February, the President of the United States of America, Nixon, visited the Great Wall at Ba Da Ling and said: "I think you have to come to this conclusion: Only a great people can build this kind of a Great Wall." He also said: "I saw a picture of the Great Wall shot by a satellite. This is a symbol of the world and ought to be a symbol of peace for mankind."

During her visit to the Great Wall on October 14th, 1986, the Queen of England, Elizabeth the second, said: "I travelled a lot of places, the Great Wall is the most beautiful one."

On the 24th of June, 2000, the Iranian President Saaid Mohammed Khattar spoke "in the name of Allah": "The ancient Great Wall marks the creation of civilization by the Chinese People throughout an endless history. The Chinese People can rely on this kind of creation to establish a flourishing civilization, become a respected people and enjoy equal right. Every country can enjoy a new world with good and superior material conditions. " The President of Argentina Fernando de la Rúa said about the Great Wall on September 13th, 2000: "Visiting mankind's greatest miracle—the Great Wall, is something I cannot put in words. The Great Wall is mankind's tie of friendship and peace."

Out of the people visiting China almost everyone wants to climb the Great Wall. Some climb it numerous times, some do all kinds of activities to explore the creativity of mankind. In September, 1994, the head of the Japanese Matsuyama Ballet, Shimizu Masao said in a speech during the Great Wall International Arts Symposium hosted by the Great Wall Academy of Arts: "The Great Wall is not only a tremendous example of architecture built by the Chinese People, it is also a dazzling treasure of the world's civilizations. The Great Wall is a universal and magnificent building, clearly visible even from a satellite. It represents all long-standing and great images all over the world." His thoughts represented those of every visitor ever climbing the Great Wall.

Experiencing more than 2500 years of a worn out Great Wall and built by the Chinese People throughout centuries, it still stands lofty and firm in the East of the World. So grand, so imposing, so powerful and letting people feel the passion of this symbolic building, there is no second one like this. While the civilization enters the 21st century and is being engulfed by the tide of globalization and information, the Great Wall as a cultural symbol remains evident. The Great Wall is not only a symbol of the Chinese People, but also of the world's civilization. As the symbol of peace for the world, the whole people benefit from this valuable cultural legacy.

Postscript · Relationship to the Great Wall

Whether they have already been there or not, for the vast majority of Chinese people, there is no other historic site able to influence and shake the mind as much as the Great Wall.

As a child, I was extremely lucky to move from the West Lake of Hangzhou to the bank of Bohai, the impregnable ShanHaiGuan in the district of Beidaihe along the sea, where I was able to perceive the life at the Sea and the Great Wall.

I still remember when I first arrived at Beidaihe, seeing the adults visiting the Great Wall that I now cannot clearly remember the kind of knowledge I had of the Great Wall back then. I also can't really remember if I thought about the meanings of the national anthem. All I remember is that I looked up at the wall as high I could hardly see its top, looked into the distance at the Great Wall I could hardly see and had this shattering feeling in my childish heart, a feeling that adults could never easily experience. This big, tall and long Great Wall left numerous questions and surprises to me as a child! When I went to the Meng Jiang Nu temple outside of Shan Hai Guan with its story about Meng Jiang Nu, which I apparently already heard in my hometown in Jiang Nan, I remember by that time being able to revere the depressed statue of Meng Jiang Nu. This feeling I cannot express in words came over me from somewhere far away and apparently let me experience another side of the Great Wall. This feeling, coexisting in endless history and the material world, was some kind of reflection of the ordinary people, including a feeling children naturally chase after. This thing I was able to feel but not to speak and didn't understand until growing up was the culture and spirit of the Great Wall.

During the period of the "Cultural Revolution" I gained my knowledge about the Great Wall through reading books and listening to great people's voices. Because of the order "Rise again like the Great Wall" of the founder of the Peoples Republic of China China Mao Zedong, the army experienced a belief deep in their heart they couldn't shake off and the Great Wall gave the a corresponding belief of strength and power in the hearts of the people. Especially the words of Mao Zedong "If you fail to reach the Wall you're a not a man", which can be recited by lots of people, arouse an emotional contagion and determine people to climb the Great Wall in order to experience the feeling of being "a man".

中国名片
CHINESE NAMECARDS

When China followed the trend of the world and under its influence started the Reform and Opening Policy and the development of the tourism in China attracted foreign articles, the mystical Great Wall became an extremely important item. Or it was just the relationship to the Great Wall that, by being responsible to receive guests for the newly established Chinese Youth Travel Agency at Qinhuang Dao, I was able to further get in contact and understand the Great Wall. At that time, every tourist from outside China or our brothers and sisters from Hongkong, Macao and Taiwan arriving at Qinhuang Dao in Beidai He without exception wanted to climb the Great Wall at Shanhai Guan. When receiving the guests I could see with my own eyes and hear with my own ears the true love and reverence the international friends and patriotic brothers and sisters revealed towards the Great Wall. Afterwards, when I had the opportunity to be in charge of the Community Service Activity "Love China, Build your Great Wall" for the city of Qinhuang Dao, I could once again intensively feel the burning patriotic enthusiasm of every Chinese people and the close attention paid by friends from every country to this great legacy of mankind.

My relationship to the Great Wall never lets me forget the May of 1984 when I followed Hua Xia Zi (pen name of Dong Yao Hui and Wu De Yu and also one month later that of Zhang Yuan Hua) and the first days of examining the Great Wall by foot, which was not only a test for the body but also the will. When I was often simultaneously using hands and feet to climb the precipitous mountains of the Great

Wall, I didn't only marvel at the people building this Wall and investing so much hardship, but also would have by any chance any words left to say something to the Great Wall?

After examining the Great Wall numerous times, I sometimes stood alone on the deserted summon of the Gobi Mountain Chains, looking around into the desolated tranquillity and feeling a predilection arising from inside the body. But seeing the Great Wall stretching itself under your feet continuously towards the far away heaven, a feeling of "one sound of cheer, thousand li's of echo" was produced, arising solitary and timidly. At this very moment, I can feel passing through time and space and get into true contact with the ancient patriotic officers and men defending the frontier and be inspired by them.

Standing on the bricks of the Great Wall, embodying everything life has to offer, on the mountains in which no men left their footmarks and looking down at the Great Wall under my feet stretching and stretching itself on the mountain ridges until it vanishes out of one's vision, one again realizes this embodiment is almost boundless. It stretches itself along the Yellow Soil Plane, the Gobi Desert far into the distance and even reaches the Sea on the other side. It's naturally never changing appearance, enveloped by a boundless canopy, stands majestically as a built with man-power and never declining high wall. Being touched by this, who could hold back his feelings of pride and solemnity of being human? As a Chinese one can again come to understand our ancestors and their approach to the unity of men and heaven and through the melting together of principles and functions of archaic truth set free even more feelings of lofty sentiment and pride.

The relationship with the Great Wall gave me again the opportunity to join in the preparations of setting up the Chinese Shanhai Guan Great Wall Research Institute and the Great Wall of China Academy. Thus being involved in all kinds of activities as disseminating, researching, protecting, maintaining and developing projects of the Great Wall as well as the exchange with my colleagues, I constantly deepened my knowledge of the Great Wall and passed this knowledge to people interested in the Great Wall, which I was glad to do. Within the last years I published some articles and books about the Great Wall and hold lectures at universities and training classes, hence putting my knowledge onto a new level.

In May 1985, when I was representing the Great Wall of China Academy arranging the draft of *Establishing a 'The Great Wall of China Academy' proposal book* in a small group, I wrote: "In the world of today, the research of the Great Wall already became a newly emerging subject. Following the call of national and international scientists for an accurate, systematic and widely covering revealing of the world's grand and dazzling cultural legacies, we propose the establishment of 'The Great Wall of China Academy' in order to unify and organize the people willing to establish a sound 'Science of the Great Wall' and by disseminating the Chinese culture, strengthen the unification of the people and provide an active role while promoting international exchange'. With the establishment of 'The Great Wall of China Academy' and the admission of the Great Wall of China onto the World Cultural Heritage List of the UNESCO, the 'Science of The Great Wall' today aroused from the ground by the initiation of Luozhe Wen and other scientists. Through intensive research, comprehensive protection, specific maintenance, and scientific dissemination of the Great Wall, the Great Wall itself already became a major topic in the 21st century.

With the relationship to the Great Wall, I wish this book *The Great Wall of China* can contribute to those people willing to understand the Great Wall and let the book be of help and inspiration to them, so that we may protect and carry on the cultural incisiveness the Great Wall reveals.

The development and driving of the economy in China's North through the Great Wall

In chinese past dynasties the construction of the Great Wall drew on a large qunatity of manpower and material ressources. After the Great Wall was built the measures of resettling people and stationing garrisons to grow their own food were put into practice in order to reinforce the defense matter of the Great Wall. Hence the agriculture and economy of Northern China developped fastly, and finally caused the Yellow River and Hetao area to become one of Northern China's rich and populous regions. Along the Great Wall emerged a certain number of specific regional, political, economical, and cultural centers.

Throughout history one can see this. Qin – and Han

– dynasty invested further in stationing garrisons and
settling people near the Great Wall. At this time there
were nearly 10 million people and soldiers. These were
scattered along the the Great Wall in many strategic
points. The large quantity of Qin- and Han - historical
objects excavated the last half century, especially the
last thirty years, indicate that at places like Wuwei
(Gansu), Suide (Shanxi), Helingeer (Inner Mongolia)
and Liaoyang (Liaoning) etc. people used oxes to
plough and iron plows. Both in northwestern Juyan
and in northeastern Liaoyang advanced agricultral
methods like farmyard manure and fertilizers were
used. Currency, weighing apparatus and measuring
instruments found along the Great Wall are like those
found inland. On stone pictures unearthed from the
Jiayu Guan tombs of Eastern Han - dynasty and

Xincheng tombs of the Wei – and Jin – period are quite exquisite depictions of the cultural and economic life at that time. The depictions of agricultural processes like plowing the earth, harrowing the earth, sowing seeds, threshing grain, protecting threshing ground etc. are very lifelike. They also reflect "drinking wells" and "silkworm bredding and mulberry growing". Furthermore printed currency excavated on the southern border of Xinjiang show chinese characters. This illustrates the close economic link between the Han – dynasty and the Western Region and the cultural interaction between them. The agriculture of the reclamation area of the region west of the Yellow River was also very developped. Dunhuang bamboo slips with chinese characters note that in the prefecture of Dunhuang there were more than 10000 units of grain including those of Shache and Shulei. This meant "the soldiers do not need money from China [to survive], but are self – suficient with grain".

Han Wudi´s success in "station garrisons to grow their own food to calm the Western Region" was honored by the latter generations as "the good method of the former generation" and "after Jin - and Wei – period there was not any generation without it".

At the beginning of Ming – dynasty garrisons were stationed in unprecedented scale. There was also a whole set of regulations, for example concerning the distribution of the accumulation of army manpower. Ordinarily, in the border district thirty percent of the army was to defend the cities and seventy percent to cultivate land. Inland twenty percent guard the land and eighty percent are stationed for cultivating. Every soldier became 50 Mu, in return he had to give plow oxes or farm implements, to plant trees or to pay rent or taxes. The basis for the troops dependend on cultivating land was established from Hongwu - till Yongle - and Xuande – period and this system became flourishing. The whole country had a standing army of approximately 1 million soldiers and 360. 000 stationed people who were regularly cultivating land. The surface area on which garrisons were stationed to grow their own food reached 8.900.000. 000 Mu in Hongwu – period, in Jiajing – period 6. 580.000.000 Mu. In the prime of that time the grand total of grain taxes yearly imposed on the border villages was 2.740.000 units of grain. Until the last years of Jiajing only the town Jizhen returned "about 100. 000 units of grain from cultivating land, and 22.000

units land, horses and silver." One can see that in the prime of that time "In fact an army of 10.000.000 soldiers needs to be maintained, but the people do not have to spend a grain of rice" is no exaggeration.

In Ming – dynasty besides the soldiers there also common people and businessmen who cultivated land at the Great Wall. At the beginning of Ming – dynasty the common peolple were mainly in the area of Beijing, Shanxi province, Shaanxi province etc. Originally there were four types of people who cultivated land at the border: the first were those from areas with big population and few land, the second were those without fields; the third were the "fallen peolple" of Yuan – dynasty or "the fallen"; the forth were people who had committed crimes or enlisted soldiers who had fled from the army.

The businessmen who cultivated land at the Grat Wall were also called salt merchants. In the first years of Ming–dynasty the businessmen were a few salt merchants among the enlisted soldiers and common people stationed to grow their own food. Ather that the government gave them salt in return for all the produced cerreals (the salt unit was "yin", in Jiazhen every big "yin" was 200 kilogramm which could be divided in 2 small "yin", each bag containing 100 kilogramm; additionally the rope of the bag weighed 40 kilogramm, so ordinary 1 "yin" was 142,5 kilogramm). The merchants used the method of buying to resell in order to obtain profit.

In Ming–dynasty because "near the border land and water were needed by the stationed troops to grow their own food, they used the same methods as inland to cultivate land". Nine strategic points along the Great Wall "were flourishing and rich, not less than the area south of the Yangtze". Ningxia became also "a small Jiangnan (area south of the Yangtze) in the north!" The first years of Ming – dynasty were a flourishing time for the soldiers, people and merchants who cultivated land at the border. Although the rules became lax afterwards, but at that time the effect on renewing the borderland economy, solving the problems of military payrolls and promoting the developpment of the borderland was still very great. Because of the defense matters required at the Great Wall in chinese history repeatedly occurred the situation that tribes of northern nomadic people settled down in the regions beyond the Grat Wall. The settlement of nomadic people near the Great Wall explains the deep influence and the advance of the peasant tiller as method of production on the nomads. This could have also been a contribution to the economic deveoppement on both sides of the Great Wall.

The construction of the Great Wall caused a stream of people and a circulation of materials towards the Great Wall on both sides. This strategic border became a place for mutual trade. The constructing of the Great Wall and implementing the policy to station troops to grow their own food and to migrate people was the basis for the establishement of the developpement of regular frontier trade between the political power of the Central Plains and the nomadic people. The reinforcement of defense matters along the Great Wall guaranteed at the same time the successful conduct of mutual trade along the Great Wall.

You may also say the restriction of the disorderly exchange of products facilitated to ensure the orderly conduct of exchanging products.

The promotion of the concentration and assimilation of the Chinese ethnic groups through the Great Wall

"2500 years, traversing 108.000 Li"the Great Wall guarded, in the course of a long history concerning military affairs, against the invasion of the backward uncivilized nomadic people. Economically it accalerated the developpement and the flourishing along the Great Wall. Culturally it formed a trend towards uniformity between inside and outside groups. Annd this all led to the accaleration of the solidification and assimilation among the Chinese peoples.

In past records the Great Wall was not a constant solide line of defense, but one which was changing becaude of the differences in strength of two sides of the Great Wall and because of the unceasingly moving of peoples. The distance between the farest northern, western or eastern point of the Great Wall and the second point north east or west was some hundred kilometers up to one thousand kilometer. This region was formed by geographical, environmental and climatical characteristics of the two great economical and cultural areas in the north and in the south. This zone is the center of what experts call "The Great Wall district".

The area which is called the "Great Wall district" is a place where more than 2000 years very different ethnis groups gatheres and melted together. Take Han – dynasty as an example, no matter if it is a place where Han – families migrated and troops were stationed, where the "Xiongnu invaded" or "the Han – people enteres the area of the Xiongnu" the area of the first mouvement was always the "Great Wall district". In Han – dynasty to back up the Great Wall, in the region west of the Yellow River the policy was put into practice to migrate people, to station garrisons to grow their own food, to set up prefectures and counties etc. The effect was that the original households there and the newly settled, like nomadic people from Central Asia, from west of the Han – empire, the Xionggu (Huns) and other people (not always Han – people) who moved there lived together in the same area and assimilated over a long period.

And at the same time for various reasons quite a number of "Han – people entered [the area ruled by] ther Xiongnu" (some of the land there was suitable for ploughing). These were, for example, plundered soldiers, soldiers who were taken prisoners, fugitives, surrenderer. In these places there was also an assimilation with local people.

Similary, northwestern and northeastern ethnic groups, like Qiang, Jie, Di, Donghu, Wuhuan preceded others in the assimilation with Han – peoplein the area of the Great Wall.

There are experts who think that since 51 AD after the southern Xiongnu turned Han, the Han – people of the farming areas of the central plaines converged with Xiongnu-people of the northern animal husbandarys. That was the beginning of the Chineses nation. Many scholars already idendify with such an opinion. In fact since the beginning of the construction of the great wall people gathered on both sides of it and begann to assimilate. The Xiongnu, Beidi, Donghu and other tribes begann to disappear after they mixed together.

After various assimilations for 100 years, the glorious Xiongnu, Donghu, Xianbei, Qiang and Jie, Di, Wuhuan ect. Were not refferd to in the cronicles afterwards. Because their absolute majority fused with Han-people or other ethnic groups, they transformed and became a new entity of people. Until Song Dynasty in the area around the great wall people again migrated in great number and fused with others. The descendents of the Xianbei – people, the Dangding, established the Western Xia – kingdom in the western part of the Great Wall. The desendents of the Donghu, the Khitan, established the Liao – kingdom in the eastern part of the Great Wall. And the Jurchen established the Jin – dynasty in the northeastern part of the Great Wall. As defense against Mongolia the Jin – dynasty built a Great Wall going from northeast to southwest (Jin boundary and trench) beyond the eastern part of the Great Wall from Qin–Han–dynasty. These three kingdoms brought about a large – scale low of population to the Great Wall area when they were founded and while they spread. Each people was mixed with others and the population of the people lived unsegregated together in the same situation. They influences each other and forgot the differences. And when the Mongolians rose and founded a state in the area of the Great Wall they marched westward and southward after stabilizing the Great Wall area. They founded the Yuan – dynasty and unified China. Later Ming – and the Manchu ruled Qing – dynasty could be established because of the mixture of Mongolians, Hui – people Semu, Manchus etc. in the Great Wall area beforehand. After they accepted the agricultural culture of the Great Plains many migrated once more in areas where different people lived. Again different ethnic groups were mixed.

In history for several thousand years, the assimilation of Chinese ethnic groups went on first of all in the Great Wall area. The foundation was the fusion of the peoples of two great cultures: the farming and handcraft culture with the animal husbandary culture. By mastering the agicultural civilization, chinese characters and culture the Han – people was the center of the multivariant interchange and fusion between different peoples. One can say that this long histiory, huge scale of assimilation with a unchanging center is unparalleled in the world.

During the unceasing assimilation process of chinese ethnic groups in the area of the Great Wall there was a kind of phenomen which is worth mentioning. After the construction of the Great Wall in Qin – dynasty all the Chinese ethnic groups in the area of the Great Wall begann to take shape. It did not if it was a time of division or unification, if China was ruled by ethnic minorities or Han – people or if there was a central or local state power. Each ethnic minority attached extrem importance to the central area of the Great Wall. It was viewed as the birth-place of their advancement and they admires and tried to imitate the Central Plains. Dating back to the origins of the ethnic groups they wished to call themselves descendents of Yan Di, Huang Di and of China. In other words the one who had power over the Central area of the Great Wall and the Central Plains had also the civilization emerging from this territory and was "advanced" and "superior". He had the authority to call himself the heir to chinese orthodox tradition, no matter if he belonged to the Han – people or any other ethnic group. This gives a full impression of the common idea of a motherland that had the different strengthened ethnic groups. It also reflects that the strong idea of a great unified chinese people was formed in the area of the Great Wall and early penetrated into the mind of the different ethnic groups.

The forerunner of the chinese democratic revolution Sun Yatsen said: " Although Qinshi Huangdi was a tyrann, he made the contribution of the Great Wall to later generations by putting into practice Dayi´s measures for water control etc. From today´s point of view, if there was not a Great Wall to guard China, then it would have been lost to the barbarians before Song – and Ming – dynasty. It would have been conquered in Chu- Han-period. Thus China would not have became prosperous and developped in Han- and Tang- dynasty, and the ethnic groups in the south would not have been assimilated. After the national assimilation and after the country was made strong and solid, altough the Mongolians once conquered China , but the Mongolians were assimilated. And the Manchus conquered China, but the Manchus were also assimilated. That wy we could conserve and multiply this big assimilating force in the first place and were not humiliated and ended early because of the northern barbarians. This is mostly so due to the Great Wall." This view of a great man is in accord with the actual historical facts. If there was not the Great Wall there would not have been a flourishing and prosperous chinese nation. And there would not have been a prosperous and developped unified country with many ethnic groups.

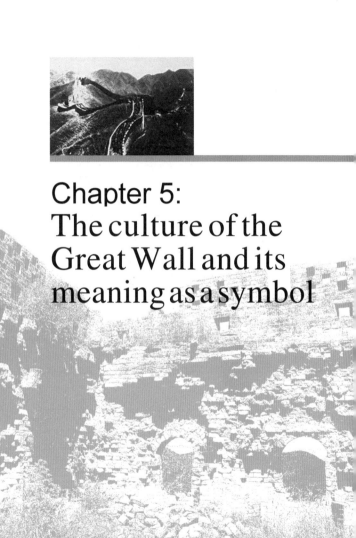

Chapter 5:
The culture of the Great Wall and its meaning as a symbol

Chapter 5:
The culture of the Great Wall
and its meaning as a symbol

The chinese Great Wall is one of the worlds most magnificient cultural legacies. Today the Great Wall is already the symbol for the Chinese nation and a famous scenis sight-seeing spot. It is already listed among the UNESCO world heritage. Because of the long construction, the material and intellectual products applied at the Great Wall are the compound system of the culture of the Great Wall. It has also long-standing, well-established, wide-ranging, profound, magnificient features and charme.

The General themes and manners of the Great Wall's culture

The culture of the Great Wall is abundant in content, all-embracing, and there is a tendency of constant evolution. However£¬because of the relative stability and uniformity of the nature and characteristics of the Great Wall, it makes the Great Wall culture general style and general theme of relative stability and unity. The general style is the tragic and the sublimity. The general theme is the great humanistic spirit of the Chinese culture and patriotism

Since the day the Great Wall was constructed, the cultural theme reflected is the great human spirit, the style is incomparably solemn. History book, "yilin" with the Qin Dynasty folk: "be cautious to lift him up when you have a boy, nurse her when you have a girl. You must have seen under the Great Wall, the bones of the dead support each other. According to Han • Jia donation of Biography, the songs of the Great Wall have never come to a stop. "Since then, not only the composition of poetry and the arts carries the same strain of the tradition, but also the most deep-rooted legend of Meng Jiangnu based on folk tales which has been circulating for more than a thousand years, poetry, opera, drama, dance, folk art, and recent modern films, songs and so on, all demonstrate such a humanistic spirit and solemnity.

By reviewing the history of Chinese poetry, one can see the Great Wall poetry is to enchant a concrete entity for a longgest time span, the largest number and the content is most abundant. Among the large group of authors of the Great Wall poetry in two thousand years, there are emperors, commoner scholars; both poetry leaders, and Taoism hermits and monks; both Han Chinese poets, and minority Mongolian, Hui, Manchu poets etc. this shows an unparalleled breadth of amplitude, from different angles, different aspects they enchant the Great Wall, reflecting a full range of the the Great Wall's heritage.

The poetry of the Great Wall relates to all aspects of the Great Wall that the content has demonstrated a significant diversity, which is one of the main reasons of the characteristics of resilience of poetry and artistic appeal of the Great Wall.

Similarly, the Great Wall proses, as in travelogues, inscriptions, Chronicle Book , Fu as well as commentary of television and movies, etc. on the Great Wall, also because of its large number of authors in different times, showing a tendency of constant evolution of the diversification of specific theme and style and Symbolism, but the general theme and the general style remain consistently from stem to stern.

Among the numerous poems of the Great Wall, some accuse the tyranny of Qin emperor, some praise that Qin built the Great Wall to bring the splendid future, some cry against the wars in support of peace, some describe as watering the horses by the side of the fountains under the Great Wall, determining to secure the borders in peace, some praise the sublimity of the mountains and rivers of the Great Wall, some describe the cold desolate borders of the Great Wall, some emphasize the plaintive wail of the widows. Many poems are involved with the appraisal of the Great Wall, some hold that the Great Wall takes on a defense of the border and civilians security, some hold that the Great Wall is vulnunerable against the enemies, some think that building the Great Wall leads to the decaying of the country, while some think that building the Great wall is a project once and for all, and some believe that the Great Wall is a mark made while the Qin emperor is incompetent, and also some believe that building the Great Wall is an act of sagacious decisions with temporary drawbacks but beneficial for ever" As of modern and contemporary times, mostly the poetry describes the Great Wall as a symbol of the Chinese nation.

If the Great Wall poems are mostly the compositions from the literates, folk stories could be the compostions from the non-literates. Among the numerous folk stories, "Meng Jiangnu" stands out to spread the longest, the most extensive and the most penetrating out of the four Chinese folk tales ("Meng Jiangnu", "Legend of Love," "The Butterfly Lovers", "White Snake").

During the forming and the spreading of Meng Jiangnu tale, not until mid-and late Ming Dynasty in China, there also rises in many places the activities of erecting temples for Meng Jiangnu. Now 6.5 km outside the Shanhaiguan at a small hill north of the Wangfu village, there stands a Meng Jiangnu temple that is said to be built in the Song dynasty, the temple, also known as "temple virgin", reconstructed in the Ming Dynasty Wanli Ershiyinian, is currently the key cultural relics protection unit in Hebei Province, with hundreds of thousands of visitors every year to be here to carry on with the incense.

For the story of Meng Jiannu, it has been widely accepted the research of the Gu Yen-wu in the late Ming and early Qing dynasties, who holds that it is originated from the story of "Qi Liang`s wife" in "Zuo

Zhuan". As in Han Dynasty, the plots of crying down the Great Wall and dying remaining unmarried were added. nevertheless, the wall mentioned in that time was not explicitly referred to the Great Wall, moreover, Qi Liang`s wife had no name.

The earliest written records that can elaborate the outline of the story of Meng Jiangnu are from " the note of Tong Xuan" quoted in "carved jade collection" during the Xuanzong time. the plots of building the Great Wall of Qin Shi Huang, Qi Liang`s fleeing to avoid service, and the meeting with Mengnu in the garden, beaten to death on the construction site after the marriage and afterward corpses built inside the walls, the seeking of mengnu, crying down the Great Wall, identifying the bones of the dead with the drops of blood etc all form up the main body of the story in latter times. It was not until between the Tang and Five Dynasties in a ditty from "Dunhuang Xieben" that the name of Meng Jiangnu was brought out, which is : "Meng Jiangnu, love(wife) of the prisoner (Qi, Yi or Fan), Mr Leung Love (Wife) , not returning after a trip to the Smoke (Yan) Hill, nobody could deliver the winter clothes after they were made, she has to deliver them on her own. " here there is an additional plot of delivering the winter clothes.

After the Tang Dynasty, through the nearly one thousand years from the Yuan Song dynasty to the Ming Qing Dynasty, the story of Meng Jiangnu continues its plots developing in the form of folk tales, such as transformation texts, precious scrolls, academic books, lyrics, dramas, songs, poems, inscriptions, the fashionable tunes and the local opera and many other art forms, all of which spread and developed among the masses. Afterwad in the story of Meng Jiangnu, a plot is added that "Qin emperor would like to marry Meng Jiangnu," however, the plot where Meng Jiangnu jumps into the sea in order to mantain her integraty after she fools the emperor who would like to take her as a concubine widely spreads in the Qing dynasty and early the Repbulic of China time, when the society is in a democratic trend of opposing despotism.

It was not until recent times that the story of Meng Jiangnu formed its basic shape. Even though the story spreads in different places with varied details and different features, the main plot remains basically the same, which is Meng Jiangnu is born, Fan (wan) Lang escapes from service, garden meeting, Fanlang arrested after marriage and sent to build the Great Wall, tired out to death and is built into the Great Wall, Meng Jiangnu delivers warm clothes from for thousands of miles, cries down hundreds(tens) of Chinese miles of the Great Wall, the emperor forces to marry, Meng Jiangnu proposes to build a grave or have the emperor offer a ceremony in person, Meng Jiangnu drowns herself etc.

The story of Meng Jiangnu spreads widely, reaching almost all over the Han areas, also in quite some fraternal ethnics areas, even to Japan and Russia and other countries.

The story reflects simple sentiments of the masses of the people toward the historical progress. The crying down the Great Wall reflects the resistance against tyranny and the labor conscription, also complaints

against the endless war. The Tang dynasty is the time
when the Meng Jiangnu story comes into form, while
in Tang Dynasty not so often do they build the Great
Wall, only constant wars continue. it is no news that
the military always marches to the frontiers, as that
Emperor Taizong is in favor of securing the borders
over building the Great Wall. But in Tang Dynasty,
especially after the mid-Tang time a number of Tang
Dynasty Frontier Poems express the discontent toward
the long-term wars and marching to the frontiers. This
is also a reflection of public sentiments, as the Tang
Dynasty poet Liu Changqing points out in the "fatigued
soldiers chapter" a resentment of " I hate the insignifi-
cant wars, which leave nothing but arrowheads all over
the Great Wall ", it could be that it is expressing the
same as that in Meng Jiangnu story, to symbolize war-

fare with a military defense project, and to express everyone`s anti-war sentiments with the crying down the Great Wall of Meng Jiangnu is a natural thing. Among the Great Wall poems from different times, all the sorrows toward building the Great Wall, and the solemnity expressed , are considered as an accusation against the tyranny and the heavy labor conscription, an extended topic of calling for peace and cherishing life. As Hui Yuan Dynasty poet Sa Douci describes directly in "Crossing Juyongguan": "Juyongguan, a strategic and grand place! Why would God not send soldiers from heaven to dispel the enemies so that the country would not need to dispatch the military. With men farming and women weaving in a peace, no warfares for ever. " Menglin, a Mongolian poet of Qing Dynasty also cries in the" Song of the Great Wall,":

There is nothing to be proud of in killing, better to kill a goat and toast it for drinking, hunting with you the deer and roe deer, we can live a secluded life as a countryside fellow everyday." Poets express a pursuit of well-being life of the majority of the people with their particular passion, applying poetic words to express their desire for peace.

The solemnity expressed in the Great Wall culture deeply reveals and reflects the unparalleled sacrifices paid by the Chinese people in the construction of the Great Wall.

The deads are incalculable during the different feudal dynasties (including the dynasties established by ethnic minorities) building the Great Wall. It is no exegeration to say " The Great Wall is built with mud and corpses lasting ten thousand Chinese miles." by

monk Guan Xiu in Late Tang Dynasty. It is harder to
calculate the money and supplies cost all over the
country. It is exactly because of the incomparably
immeasurable sacrifice of the Chinese people in
building the Great Wall that the Chinese people remember it for generations, returning with tragic poems and stories of Meng Jiangnu to express the Chinese humanism in opposition to the war and tyranny,
in favor of peace, life. Therefore, the descendants of
those who built the Great Wall, hold reverent sentiments with a distant memory from the bottom of their
soul, such sentiments, are the source to cohere the
general style and the general theme of the Great Wall
culture, like fire, flows quietly usually in the depths
of the earth, preparing silently, once it reaches the
critical moments concerning the survival of the nation

(for example, the nation's anti-Japanese war) it would break out, soaring, becoming fire that can burn down the wilderness, calling each indignant Chinese, " to build our flesh and blood into our new Great Wall", to defend the beautiful homes and defend the great motherland, and to defend the sacred honor of the Chinese nation, to inspire for the utmost patriotism, to create significant heroic deeds.

Among the Poems of the ancient Great Wall, despite the diferences of authors' understandings on functions of the Great Wall, no one denies the magnificent grandness of the Great Wall by reserving their compliments on the particular magnificent and grand sceneries:" Sunrise upon Xihai, grandness appears more splendid with the wind in the frontier fortress, shining upon the mountains and gate passes, appearing in indescribable desolation. "(Tang• Cui Rong," Guan Shanyue "), " The Great Wall grandly starts from Tiao River, zigzagging nine thousand Chinese miles "(Yuan • Zhou Quan "The Great Wall ")," Moon that ever shone upon the Qin Dynasty hangs in the air like a lunar bow, the Yellow River links up the gate passes of Han Dynasty like a ribbon. "(Ming • Yang Shen," Saiheng Zhegu"), " Yellow birds fly from the valley to the trees, egrets fly over the mountains in the distance, the beautiful cloak is relieved against the peach blossom under the sunshine , branches riding the wind hang on the saddle. " (Ming • Gao Wei, "Return after victory to Daomaguan") "The great Wall zigzags for so long that it links up Zhao,Wei, Youzhou and Yan. It offers a firm defense, standing grandly on the mountains for a thousand years. The Great Wall measures more than ten thousand Chinese miles, standing high in confrontation with the clouds, the mountains are disconnected and staggered, but the wall reamins continuous, linking to the sky in the west, the sea in the east. "(Qing • Xu Sun Tsuen,"Song under the Great Wall")" Whipping the rocks to where the mountains and the coulds link up, overviewing Youzhou and bingzhou.it reaches the mountains in Bohai to the east, and the upper stream of Yellow River to the west, with the sunset shining upon it. under a clear sky, the outpost is very often put under the central political administration, in peace time, no smoke comes out of the beacon tower, after the Great Wall strongholds, the mountains appear very grand (Kang Youwei, stepping on the Great Wall) and one of the founders of the People's

Republic of China, Mao Zedong who wrote : " He who does not reach the Great Wall is not a true man " concisely and skillfully reflected the splendor of the cultural style and bold spirit of the Great Wall. It is this style and spirit that has attracted millions of people, including many foreigners to experience the charm of the Great Wall, to affirm the human power to be a future "hero."

Among the numerous poetries of the Great Wall, to a large extent the splendor of the cultural style of the Great Wall demonstrated lies in the aesthetic concepts of the Great Wall. It is for the magnificence of the Great Wall, the perfect combination of the Great Wall and the nature, and the human creativity reflected by the Great Wall that it endows The Great Wall of eternal significance of noblity and sublime.

As of a comprehension of the point of views, cultural phenomena, there exists positive and negative views toward the functioning of the national security of the Great Wall in history, however, this does not shake the essence of the Great Wall, on the contrary, it emphasizes the general theme of the Great Wall culture from both positive and negative aspects, distinguishing the highlight of the humanism in the Great Wall culture. It equals to supporting the justice, opposing to the invasion, maintaining the peace by supporting the view of the security function of the Great Wall, and it equals to denying tyranny, complimenting life, desiring for peace. These two views are unified in the profound stretches of the great virtue of Chinese humanism.

图书在版编目（ＣＩＰ）数据

长城 The Great Wall / 孙志生著；(英) 大卫译.—北京：新星出版社，2010.12
（中国名片丛书）
ISBN 978-7-80225-773-3

Ⅰ．长… Ⅱ.①孙…②大… Ⅲ.长城－简介－英文 Ⅳ.K928.77

中国版本图书馆CIP 数据核字（2009）第175871 号

The Great Wall

作　　者：孙志生
翻　　译：(英) 大卫

责任编辑：朴文姬
责任印制：韦　舰
装帧设计：zhengmei正美
　　　　　书籍装帧设计组 010-64003130
出版发行：新星出版社
出 版 人：谢　刚
社　　址：北京市西城区车公庄大街丙 3 号楼　　100044
网　　址：www.newstarpress.com
电　　话：010-88310888
传　　真：010-88310899
法律顾问：北京市大成律师事务所
读者服务：010-88310800　service@newstarpress.com
邮购地址：北京市西城区车公庄大街丙 3 号楼　　100044
印　　刷：北京中科印刷有限公司
开　　本：880 × 1230　1/16
印　　张：16.5
字　　数：128 千字
版　　次：2010 年 12 月第一版　　2010 年 12 月第一次印刷
书　　号：ISBN 978-7-80225-773-3
定　　价：USD19.80